WITHDRAWN

EC -- 2006

385.097
L10

illinois terminal

In Color

VOLUME I

by Gordon E. Lloyd

Copyright © 1998
Morning Sun Books, Inc.

All rights reserved. This book may not be reproduced in part or in whole without written permission from the publisher, except in the case of brief quotations or reproductions of the cover for the purposes of review.

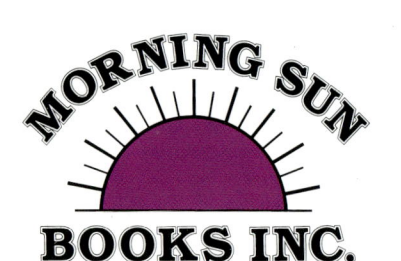

Published by
Morning Sun Books, Inc.

9 Pheasant Lane
Scotch Plains, NJ 07076

Library of Congress
Catalog Card No. 98-065948

First Printing
ISBN 1-58248-000-1

Color separation and printing by
The Kutztown Publishing Co., Inc.
Kutztown, Pennsylvania

DEDICATION

This volume is dedicated to Janet, my wife and helpmate of 45 years.

ACKNOWLEDGMENTS

The Illinois Terminal System was a vast operation, covering much of central Illinois, with a lifespan of almost 60 years. To give a complete photographic coverage of the system, even in its declining years, would have been a formidable task. Unfortunately, many of the photos in my personal collection are in black and white format and consequently of no use in an all-color book.

Much of the content of this book is the result of almost weekly trips out of Chicago "downstate", weather permitting. Since my color photography did not begin until the early 1950s, the extent of my IT color coverage is limited. On the brighter side, the photos included in this book do show both the electric and diesel operations, the orange and blue eras of interurban paint schemes, and the short-lived STREAMLINER era. Not included, because they disappeared prior to 1940, are the sleeper trains, especially the OWL, which operated between Peoria and St. Louis from 1908 to 1940. The various small town streetcar systems operated by IT likewise were discontinued prior to the advent of color film, so they could not be included.

My close and long time friend, Don Idarius, accompanied me on most of the trips illustrated in this volume. Other companions on IT visits, following and photographing the cars by automobile, or actually riding on the line in one of their impressive interurban cars, included Joe Diaz, Bob Gibson, and the late Jim Buckley. My thanks to all of these friends for sharing their camaraderie during those golden days. It was a lot of fun.

In later years, my wife, sons, and daughters endured what to them often was boredom, as I waited trackside for a speeding limited to come by. This volume will, hopefully, prove that it was all worth their investment in time away from the beach. Of course, a special thanks to Bob Yanosey for his help and counsel and to Bill Volkmer, who proofread and edited the manuscript.

I. ILLINOIS TERMINAL HISTORICAL OVERVIEW

From the onset, it should be made clear that the creation of the Illinois Terminal Railroad along with its predecessors was not a random act. Neither was it a get rich scheme, as were so many other interurbans that were considered to be "typical". The first line destined to later become a part of the ITS was the Danville, Paxton and Northern Railroad, incorporated in 1899. Its initial construction provided a link between Danville, in eastern Illinois, with Georgetown, Homer, and Ridge Farm to the south. It then began heading southwesterly with a line to Catlin, IL, 6.4 miles away. In 1903, the DP&N was acquired by the Danville, Urbana and Champaign Railway Co. connecting Danville with Urbana, a distance of 31 miles.

Building then commenced from Springfield up to Decatur followed in 1907 by a segment from Springfield to Staunton. When the first interurban building boom ended in 1907, the St. Louis and Northeastern RR was added to the complex. Work was also being undertaken from Peoria south to Decatur. Belt lines were built around Springfield and Edwardsville in order to facilitate the movement of carload freight a farsighted move never simulated by the neighboring Indiana interurban lines. In 1907, the construction of new lines went into a hiatus as the industry began its long and painful decline.

Following World War I the IT discovered that there existed a cheaper alternative to more interurban construction. That was to purchase existing paralleling railroads coming with the built-in advantage of already having freight shipping industries located along the lines. This was particularly the case in the St. Louis area, especially on the Illinois side of the Mississippi River. In the early 1920s several aquisitions occurred, but expansion stopped during the Depression, then resumed in the late 1930s when economic good times returned. By 1940, the Illinois Terminal Railroad, as we came to know it, was basically complete.

Around 1910, the name "Illinois Traction System" came into general use for the great number of smaller lines that had been unified by the McKinley management. As properties in and around St. Louis and Alton came under IT control (1937) the formal name was changed to Illinois Terminal System, a name which endured until shortly after electric passenger service ended in 1956. Briefly, the name of the railroad was changed to Illinois-Missouri Terminal RR, and then, on June 25, 1956 the Illinois Terminal name was readopted, as the IT was purchased by a consortium of Class I railroads. The IT began running on trackage rights over the lines of its owners (B&O, C&EI, CB&Q, GM&O, L&M (C&NW), IC, Wabash, NYC and CRI&P) as well as small portions of its own line. Much of the former IT electrified interurban trackage was ripped up following cessation of passenger service. This method of operation continued until late in 1981 when what remained of the system, the locomotive fleet in particular, was purchased by the Norfolk and Western. IT was merged into the N&W system already consisting of the merged Wabash and Nickel Plate railroads.

One significant IT landmark that remained in place was the McKinley Bridge over the Mississippi River on the north side of St. Louis. Completed in 1910, four years after service had begun to Granite City, this was the only railroad bridge over that river owned by a single railroad. it was a significant asset to the N&W, providing access to the second largest railroad complex in the United States, St. Louis, where connections to the west and southwest were made over a variety of railroad lines.

II. THE PRAIRIE STATE'S "OWN" INTERURBAN

Illinois, the Prairie State, had many miles of interurban line. The so-called "Insull" lines, in the Chicago area have been covered in my previous Morning Sun book, *The Insull Chicago Interurbans CA&E, CNS&M, CSS&SB, in Color*. These famous lines were examples of what an interurban operation could be. In point of fact, they were not what we would call "typical" interurbans when compared with those in the rest of the nation. Multiple car train operation, high grade rights-of-way, and heavy commuter traffic characterized those lines.

Downstate Illinois had is own unique style of interurban. The Illinois Traction System, or, as it later became known, the Illinois Terminal Railroad System, was also not your "typical" interurban. Rather, the IT amounted to a steam railroad that chose electrification over steam for motive power. Long freight trains powered by electric, steam, and finally diesel locomotives augmented by electrically powered interurban-style passenger cars characterized the IT system. Its predominately rural setting, in the heartland of Illinois was what brought it close to the roots of the state. It was intimately a part of the agricultural base of the state, largely dependent upon the crops emanating from the rich Illinois soil. In later years, the railroad was also able to build a substantial base moving industrial products as well.

Fans and students of the electric railways of America are keenly aware of the paralleling development of electric railways and automotive technology and infrastructure. Some say that if the interurban concept had come along ten years after it did, it never would have happened because it would have been redundant. Only a fraction of the peak mileage would have been built. Another matter was the application of electric power to urban transportation in the 1890s. Here the need to convert the means for movement of people from horse drawn, or cable cars, to electric propulsion was persuasive. Immediate and sizable savings could be realized by conversion to electric propulsion.

The principal obstacle to interurban promotion and expansion, even in the early part of the 20th century was the innate desire of many of the rural populace to own a family automobile. Their perceived need was boosted by seemingly endless advertising by the automobile manufacturers which emphasized "neighbor envy" in order to sell more autos, more often, of larger and more expensive variety. Once the auto buyer had made the initial investment it was difficult to leave his car at home and use public transportation, even to go to work.

Although freight formed the backbone of the ITC operation, the orange, later painted blue, interurban cars connected the small Illinois hamlets, with larger Illinois cities of Peoria, Springfield, Danville, and Champaign-Urbana, with the railroad's anchor city, St. Louis, MO. These cars had the appeal that the freights lacked. The fact that the electric operation lasted until the mid-1950s, long after most other interurban operations had succumbed to highway traffic, was a tribute to the policies of the original planners of the railroad.

As with most business enterprises, the formation and ultimate success of the Illinois Terminal could be attributed largely to the efforts on one man. That man was William Brown McKinley. There is often confusion between the W.B. McKinley of IT fame and the 27th President of the United States William McKinley, who was assassinated in Buffalo on September 6, 1901. The President was born in Niles, Ohio in 1843. The IT McKinley was thirteen years younger, born in Petersburg, Illinois, September 5, 1856. Both McKinleys served two unconnected terms in the U.S. House of Representatives and Senate, and both were Republicans. While the President McKinley's aspirations were mainly political, having served as Governor of Ohio in addition to his two terms as a Congressman, William Brown McKinley's political interests were secondary to his empire building interests, principally in the areas of transportation and power utilities. His career encompassed transit, beginning with the Champaign-Urbana Horse Railway in 1884, and culminating with the owning or controlling of 23 separate transit properties, some as far away as Omaha, Nebraska, Topeka and Wichita, Kansas, along with numerous electric, gas, and water utility companies. Unlike Mr. Insull of Chicago fame, Mr. McKinley was never involved in scandals and was considered a solid product and credit to the Prairie State.

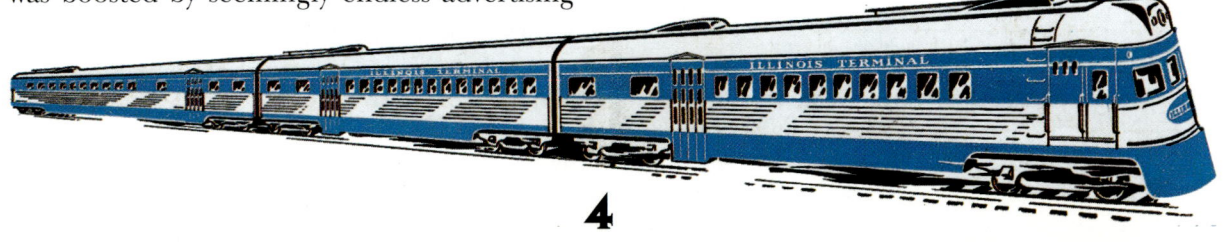

4

III. PASSENGER OPERATIONS

Before we photographically examine the IT in greater detail, perhaps it would be useful to the reader if we profile the physical aspects of the railroad. It was primarily a single track railroad powered by 650 volts DC in overhead wire. Track ballast was largely made up of cinders from steam locomotives and power plant boilers. In addition to the main line trackage, there was an extensive switching operation in Illinois within the Alton-East St. Louis area. It was steam powered, but was converted to diesel-electric in the late 1940s. In 1950, there was also an extensive suburban commuter service from St. Louis to Granite City, Illinois, a steel mill town.

Passenger service, which was held to a high performance level by the ITC right up to the end of electrified operation, was characterized by posh stations in the major cities that rivaled and indeed often surpassed those of the competing steam railroads. The beautiful station in Peoria still stands and is used by the Peoria Police Department for its headquarters. Other new stations were built over the years, notably in Springfield and Decatur. The "capstone" of these modern stations was the beautiful St. Louis IT terminal. In addition to being a work of art, it was utilitarian, being reached by an elevated and subsurface line that connected the McKinley Bridge to the station. It remained in service until 1956. This was the only station in St. Louis to accommodate a single railroad, other than the Wabash suburban station at Delmar. All other passenger trains entering St. Louis used Union Station, on the premier railroad stations in the nation. The IT St. Louis station was also the western terminal of the Granite City-St. Louis local service that was modernized with PCC cars in 1948 and abandoned ten years later, in 1958.

The Illinois Terminal now exists in the minds of those who rode it and possibly more vividly in the memories of those who cherish it as an Icon. Our readers should remember that the Indiana Railroad, the Lake Shore Electric, the Cincinnati and Lake Erie, and the Sacramento Northern were all gone in the early 1940s or late 1930s. The Chicago interurbans survived World War II and made great contributions to victory in the war, but they were more suburban operations than was the Illinois Terminal. In reality it was as close as one could come in 1943 to what a true interurban should be that could be found on the continent. One would expect that fans of the various Iowa interurban lines would want to dispute that statement.

Let me offer an image of the ITC that has remained in my mind for over 54 years.

I was inducted into the US Army in March, 1943. Arriving at Union Station in Chicago, a group of we "civilians" were about to begin the experience of our lives. We boarded a CB&Q train. It could not be called a troop train, as although we had been inducted into the US Army, we were still for all intents and purposes, civilians. The train took us through familiar territory up to Camp Grant, IL, near Rockford. Army clothing was issued, as well as a number of tests, etc. After a couple of days of basic indoctrination, we and our heavy barracks bags went down to the train boarding location. We boarded the C&NW suburban cars, still equipped with gas lights, and proceeded back to the yards behind Union Station in Chicago. Finally we were again under way. This time on the ALTON LIMITED. (later GM&O and still later ICG). On the fabled Train #1, the ALTON LIMITED. It was from the windows of this train that I had my first glimpse of the Illinois Terminal. It was about 12:45 PM as #1 cleared the interlocking north of Lincoln, IL that I saw a two car IT train (probably #93, the ILLMO LIMITED) to the left side of our train. The Conductor was positioning the pole on the motor car to the wire as the drizzling rain came down. This is one of the images that I will forever remember. Most of the men on that train could not have cared less, but to me, this was the legendary ITC, a company that I had always dreamed of riding, but had never seen until that instant.

IT passenger service operated well into its last decade with several passenger cars built between 1907 and 1914 by the St. Louis Car Company and others. Cars used on the main Peoria-St. Louis service were among the first interurban cars to be air conditioned in the country. Many received modern walk-over seating, but they were still of the "old order", when compared to the modern streamlined trains that the GM&O, IC and Wabash offered their patrons, in direct competition with the IT.

After the war the IT had recognized the modernization activities of the Chicago interurban lines. The CA&E had received ten new cars in 1946, the CSS&SB had lengthened, air-conditioned, and modernized many of their passenger cars and the CNS&M had been operating their fabled ELECTROLINERS on fast schedules since 1941. Technology advances in interurban car building had been impeded as the traction industry went into decline, but they had not stopped altogether. Following dramatic traffic increases as a result of World War II, IT believed that they could retain a good portion of that business with modern but not rebuilt equipment. St. Louis Car Co., which had built the majority of the IT passenger equipment was the logical builder of choice for modern cars. St. Louis had designed and built the ELECTROLINERS as well as the CA&E modern cars. The *Streamliner* design that they came up with in 1947 pleased some, but disappointed others.

The *Streamliners* consisted of two three-car trains and one two-car train and all had buffet-parlor cars in their consists. Their interiors were the equal of any class one road car of the late 1940s, but the exterior design was not as dramatic as that of the distinctive ELECTROLINERS that were seven years older.

It was that exterior design that caused caustic observers to exclaim, "They look just like a 1929 model gas electric car!" Probably that was a correct assessment,. The "shovel nose" of those cars duplicated the rebuilding of some of the older gas-electric equipment on the steam roads. The balance of the car, however, was "state-of-the-art". Having ridden them, in both coach and parlor configurations, I found they had the ride and seating comfort equal to any steam road car. Unfortunately, they were not able to keep the passenger business on IT rails. The decline in ridership continued. The two car CITY OF DECATUR was holding down the premier Decatur-Springfield-St. Louis service in the hope of luring patrons from the Wabash Railroad. The Wabash Streamliner BLUE BIRD, its equally swank BANNER BLUE and the CANNONBALL all offered similar service between Decatur and St. Louis over a shorter and faster route. The CITY OF DECATUR was transferred to Peoria-Springfield-St. Louis service in June of 1950. The three-car *Streamliners*, FORT CREVE COEUR and MOUND CITY also performed a similar service, Peoria to St. Louis, a route having no direct class-one road passenger competition. On November 12, 1950 the parlor-buffet cars were withdrawn from all runs, thus ending all pretensions of providing deluxe service on the IT. The now two-car nameless trains soon became one car operations as passengers left and went to their cars or to paralleling buses. Clearly the IT was getting out of the passenger business.

IV. FREIGHT OPERATIONS

Probably no electric railroad was more aggressive in soliciting carload freight movements over its lines than was the Illinois Terminal. In 1950 it had "on-line" and "off-line" salesmen in 21 cities. To a greater degree than most interurbans, the IT could be worked into sensible transcontinental routings. The ITC was truly a part of the logical US railroad map. It handled cars from wherever to the ultimate destination with the efficiency that was a part of the "normal" railroad service.

With reference to freight car supply, the ITC contributed its normal or fair share. Its primary attention was to its on-line shippers. In 1966 IT owned 2,357 cars. Box cars and covered hoppers constituted the bulk of the cars, but it also was relatively "heavy" in the number of gondola cars on its roster. For a short line railroad, it gave its fair share to the national car fleet. No other electric interurban company had as many cars in interchange service. The planning of William McKinley was evident in where the ITC rated in car availability.

From an historical prospective, the ITC leaning toward carload freight traffic came early in the history of the line. While other interurbans were plagued with the problem of what to do when passenger revenues declined, the ITC had focused long before that time on how to increase freight revenue. The company was far ahead of the times. No one had anticipated the effect of the motor truck, once the highways were improved from mud-rutted trails to federal or state supported, all-weather highways. The foresight of the ITC, under McKinley management, to build belt lines around the major Illinois cities, was of inestimable value as the trend away from passenger traffic and towards freight haulage became the prime objective of ITC Management.

It is regrettably true that no one can really foresee the future. The management of the ITC was as informed as the management of other Class 1 railroads. Perhaps that is not saying too much. We have seen, with backward vision being clearly more accurate than what could be forecasted for the future, it is difficult to see a trend. One only has to recall that the Pennsylvania Railroad was building new less-than-carload lot (LCL) transfer buildings in Pittsburgh as late as 1952, at a time when the LCL business had clearly been lost forever, to trucks. Such is an evaluation of railroad "vision". Hindsight is always 20-20.

In an impressive brochure compiled by Elmer E. Kester, Passenger Traffic Manager for the ITC, published in April, 1947, there was a prophetic message about the decentralization of industry in the United States. Although accurate, the decentralization predicted by Mr. Kester did not especially redound to the benefit of the railroads. Rather, the motor carrier has been the prime beneficiary of that decentralization trend. A good prediction, but the effect was not what the rail industry had predicted or wanted.

ITS freight operations began with express movements carried in the baggage section of passenger motor cars. Virtually 100% of the ITS passenger interurban cars were equipped with a baggage section in the front. Revenue from such operations was modest, but it was a beginning. The goal of the ITC was to handle standard railroad cars in local and in interchange service.

As we have noted, the IT constructed belt lines around the larger cities on its lines and managed to "mollify" the smaller cities and towns into allowing standard steam road cars to be hauled down their main streets. Originally, car interchange with an interurban line was shunned by the steam roads, as electric lines were considered arch-enemies. The IT, however, was not to be defeated by any arguments. It went to work on the smaller steam lines first. By 1909 it had worked out interchange arrangements with the C&EI, CRI&P, and the St. Louis-San Francisco (FRISCO). A few years later, interchange was effected with the Terminal Railroad of St. Louis (TRRA). It was then just a matter of time until all of the neighboring roads fell into line. The TRRA was jointly owned by larger railroads entering St. Louis, so if it could interchange with IT, why not with its owners? Car interchange was difficult on the Decatur to Mackinaw Junction line (via Bloomington), but this was due to track curvature, not due to agreement reasons.

Power for the first freight trains was with Class "A" steeple cab locomotives. Later, the Class "B" and "C" locomotives were the primary power for freight trains. In 1940, the big Class "D" locomotives powered hot-shot freights and continued until the first road diesels appeared on the property in 1953. They handled the time freights, later working the locals and switching service as the electric locos were withdrawn from service. A dividend from diesel operation that was not appreciated, was their "pounding of the light interurban rail." This problem could only be alleviated by laying heavier rail. The obvious antidote to this was to abandon the line and obtain trackage rights over paralleling roads.

It should be mentioned that IT operated the switching trackage in the Alton-St. Louis area by steam locomotives, and by combination electric-diesel locomotives. Diesel operation on the IT began when some industries located along the line or grew and desired a rail connection, but did not want trolley wires on their property. The very busy IT switching area to the east of E. St. Louis on the Illinois side of the Mississippi was worked by steam power, primarily locomotives with the 2-6-0 wheel arrangement. There was also a scattering of 2-8-0s and 0-8-0s. These were generally unsafe in the petroleum refining and chemical processing areas of the switching operations. In addition, steam power had environmental objections from some people, yes, even then!

Gradually as straight electric freight power became older and harder to repair, the decision was made to operate the IT as a diesel, freight only, railroad. Diesels began to appear on the property in greater numbers. Early diesels were in the B-B wheel configuration, later power consisted of C-C six motor units.

V. SMALLER OPERATIONS OF THE ITC AND ILLINOIS VALLEY DIVISION

Some of the smaller operations of the ITC came from the purchase of independent railroads. One such oddity was the line between Alton and Grafton, originally built in the 1880s. Service was provided by a flanged wheel rail bus until the relatively late date of May, 1953. The maze of switching tracks in the East St. Louis-Granite City area were a mix of steam and electric operations until they were dieselized in the 1950s.

The Illinois Valley Division of the IT was a different matter. The line was originally projected from De Pue, Illinois on the west to Joliet, on the east. Also a branch ran south from Ottawa to Streator. A link was proposed between the "Valley Division" and the other ITC lines terminating at Peoria. It was also planned to establish a Chicago-Peoria-Springfield-St. Louis service. Cars between Joliet and Chicago would be run on the Chicago-Joliet Electric Railway, an Insull-controlled property. It was to operate as a passenger operation, with limited freight and later be upgraded for carload freight. The line would not have been competitive, time wise for through traffic to St. Louis because of the side-of-the-road nature of the Valley Division and numerous slow running portions caused by curving track. It would have had a hard time securing passenger business from Chicago to its major scenic attraction, "Starved Rock State Park" because of the slow streetcar connections of the Chicago Surface Lines on Archer and Cicero Avenues plus the equally "lazy" schedules of the Chicago and Joliet Electric Ry.

The Valley Division was recognized as a loser and was abandoned in the mid-1930s, before its operation could be recorded on color film.

ITC had some suburban operations, most notably the St. Louis-Granite City run, which was ultimately operated in part by multiple-unit PCC cars. Other suburban runs were Peoria-Morton, East St. Louis-Edwardsville, Danville-Hilery-Georgetown and Danville-Catlin. All were gone by 1940. Staunton to Hillsboro was a shuttle operation. During WW II, the ITC operated locomotive hauled ex-New York City "L" cars from Decatur to Illiopolis and Springfield to Illiopolis. This operation, designed to save automobiles and fuel, was terminated as hostilities ended.

ITC also operated streetcars in several downstate cities. Among them were Danville, Decatur, and Champaign-Urbana. These operations were ultimately sold to National City Lines who promptly converted the rail lines to bus operation.

VI. THE LONGEST INTERURBAN TRIP

The question of what was the longest interurban trip that one could take over a single company's route seems to have deviled the interurban aficionado community for many years. It is generally known that the long route of the Sacramento Northern from Oakland to Chico, CA was one of the most varied and interesting of all single line electric railway runs. It was 184.6 miles in length and featured dining and observation car service between the two cities. This notable run was not the longest that one could take on a single ownership interurban. The Cincinnati and Lake Erie run from Cincinnati to Toledo and Detroit would certainly qualify in the competition.

The Illinois Terminal should also be considered. The Danville-Springfield line was 127 miles of single track and if one transferred at Springfield for the journey north to Peoria, an additional 73 miles was added to the trip for a total of 195 miles. If the traveler was going to St. Louis, it was 122+88 or a total of 210 miles. Such trips were not unusual in the glory days of the interurban. Moreover, the IT offered dining service on the Springfield-St. Louis runs as well as sleepers until 1940 from Peoria to St. Louis.

The above comparisons were useful only to armchair surveyors of the interurban scene as the relevance of who had the longer line is a moot point, of value only to those who feel good in expounding such knowledge.

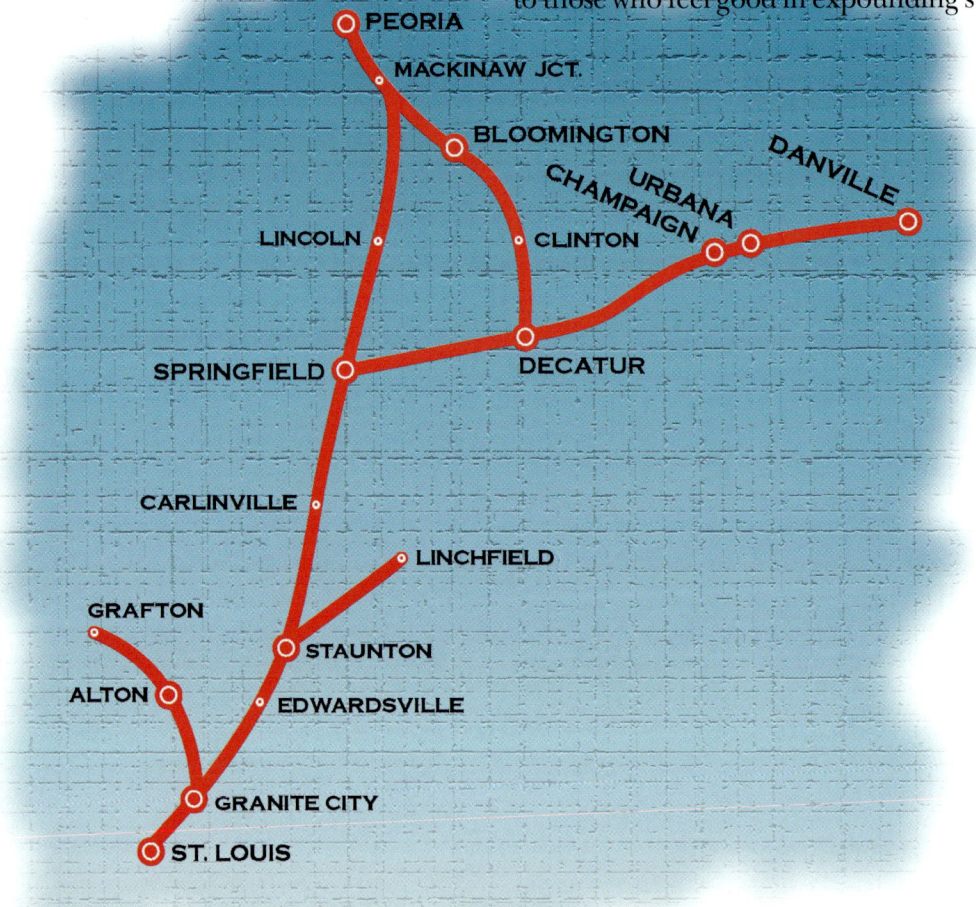

SIGNIFICANT EVENTS IN THE LAST YEARS OF IT PASSENGER OPERATION - 1948 TO 1958

NOVEMBER 7, 1948	CITY OF DECATUR, IT's first *Streamliner* set entered revenue service. Decatur-St. Louis, 137 mile trip. Trains cannot operate into Peoria because of tight curves and pilots striking pavement in dips.
JANUARY 1, 1949	All *Streamliners* withdrawn from service and shipped back to St. Louis Car Company for debugging.
MAY, 1949	All three sets of *Streamliners* are back in service.
NOVEMBER, 1949	Eight MU equipped PCC cars, 450-457 enter service on the St. Louis-Granite City streetcar line. IT's last new cars, they had been on order since 1946.
JANUARY 15, 1950	Peoria-East Peoria through trains are discontinued because of a combination of clearance problems with the new trains and high bridge maintenance costs over the Illinois River. A shuttle car provides service pending permission to abandon.
JUNE 8, 1950	Shuttle service is abandoned. Buses transfer passengers from Peoria.
AUGUST 17, 1950	*Streamliner* CITY OF DECATUR terminated. Replaced by older equipment.
APRIL 26, 1952	Line abandoned between Danville and Watkins. Cars 264, 284 & 285 receive a front pole for backing operation east of Ogden.
FEBRUARY 21, 1953	Line is abandoned from Mackinaw Junction to Forsythe (67 miles) ending service from E. Peoria to Decatur.
APRIL 25, 1953	Six mile shuttle from Decatur to Forsythe is abandoned.
MAY 23, 1953	Alton passenger service is terminated. Rail bus to Grafton discontinued also. Fifteen mile Grafton line is abandoned.
JUNE 11, 1955	Last train from Champaign to Decatur and from E. Peoria to Springfield. Car 277 is last car from E. Peoria.
MARCH 3, 1956	Last train from Springfield to St. Louis and return. 284-530-531 are last cars to run.
JUNE 22, 1958	1 AM last streetcar pulls into St. Louis, MO ending all IT passenger service and all streetcar service in the state of Illinois.

ABANDONMENTS AFTER 1958

DECEMBER 1, 1959	Decatur to Springfield
APRIL 30, 1961	De Long to Urbana
OCTOBER 16, 1961	Decatur to Champaign
APRIL 1, 1962	Lincoln to Sherman
AUGUST 1, 1966	East Peoria to Morton
SEPTEMBER 22, 1968	Springfield to Nilewood
AUGUST 6, 1977	Allentown to Lincoln

DIESEL ROSTER

ORIG. NUMBERS	RENUMBER NEW NUMBERS	BUILDER	DATE	MODEL
700-705	1001-1008	Alco	1948	S-2
706-711	1007-1012	Alco	1950	S-2
751-752	1051-1052	Alco	1948	RS-1
753	1053	Alco	1948	RS-1
754-756	1054-1056	Alco	1950	RS-1
725	801	EMD	1950	SW8
776-786	1201-1212	EMD	1955	SW1200
	1220-1221	EMD	1950	SW7
	1507	EMD	1949	F7B (ex-RF&P)
	1508	EMD	1950	F7B (ex-RF&P)
1600-1605	1501-1506	EMD	1953	GP7
	3419	EMD	1954	GP9
	1750	EMD	1952	GP7u
	1509-1515	EMD	1970	SW1500
	2001-2004	EMD	1977	GP38-2
	2008-2009	EMD	1970	GP20 (ex-UP)
	2301-2306	EMD	1989	SD39

SUMMARY OF LATER YEARS EQUIPMENT

ELECTRIC CAR ROSTER

CAR NUMBERS	BUILDER	DATE	NOTES
PASSENGER CARS			
240	American Car & Foundry	1908	
241	"	1908	
242-247	"	1908	
248-249	"	1908	
250-257	"	1904	
258-259	St. Louis Car Co.	1906	
260-264	Danville Car Co.	1911	
270	Niles Car Co. for CD&M	1906	
271	Holland Car for CD&M	1903	
273-283	St. Louis Car Co.	1913	
284-285	"	1914	
TRAILERS			
510-514	St. Louis Car Co.	1911	Reserved Seats
515	"	1913	"
***STREAMLINER* CARS**			
300-302	St. Louis Car Co.	1948	
330-331	"	1948	
350-352	"	1948	
SUBURBAN & PCC CARS			
450-457	St. Louis Car Co.	1949	PCC
404-415	"	1924	Ex CO&P
470-473	"	1924	Center Entrance
100-104	American Car Co.	1917	"
120-123	E. St. Louis & Suburban	1924	"
LOCOMOTIVES			**CLASS**
1550-1558	Danville Car Co.	1904-07	A
1559-1566	Alco GE	1907	B
1567-1598	ITC - Decatur Shop	1914-26	C
70-74	ITC Decatur Shop	1940-42	D

DANVILLE - DECATUR - SPRINGFIELD LINE

The Danville to Springfield line was 121 miles in length operating in an east-west oriented direction, Danville being on the east. Danville was where the McKinley Illinois Traction System was born. Intermediate stations were Champaign, Urbana, and Decatur. The city operations around Danville opened in 1901, the interurban line through to Decatur in 1907. Service was abandoned on the Danville end beginning in April 1952, and finishing with the Champaign to Decatur segment on June 11, 1955. Freight traffic was never terribly important on this line and it too was discontinued immediately following the cessation of passenger services.

DANVILLE

Essential parts of every human endeavor are a beginning and an ending. In the case of the Illinois Traction System, the beginning place was Danville, Illinois, on the extreme eastern border of the state. The first car operated there on September 16, 1901, ten days following the assassination of President William McKinley. At that time, the first passenger car left downtown Danville, bound for the village of Westville, some 19 miles south of town. We too begin our color tour of the IT at Danville, only by October 31, 1951, the IT stood for Illinois Terminal Railroad Company. A three-car special train has just arrived from Springfield with a capacity load of Shriners enroute to a Masonic conclave in the downtown area.

About seven weeks previous, in September, 1951, car 285 is seen arriving from a 121 mile run that originated in Springfield. It will soon depart back to Springfield as train 77 furnishing 3 1/2 hours of pure "traction delight".

11

JAILHOUSE BLUES

Shortly after departing the Danville terminal, the track took a curve in front of the Vermilion County jail. The residents of this "hotel with bars" probably enjoyed witnessing the passage of the trains as an interesting diversion to their otherwise colorless day. In this instance, a two car special, consisting of combine 277 and trailer 535 provided the activity. The 277 would wind up at the Illinois Railway Museum, so that future generations could enjoy.

LONE CLASS B SURVIVOR

The Illinois Power Co. utilized a former IT box motor, formerly the IT 1566 at their power plant west of Danville. Here, on August 31, 1957, after all other electrified rail operation had ceased, the B class motor awaits a call to switch another set of hoppers into the plant. The continued tenure of the motor was to be short lived.

Danville was never very important as a freight generator to the IT, because the city was served by three steam railroads, the Wabash, New York Central (Big Four), and the Chicago and Eastern Illinois. Passengers were another story, for in 1943, there were still six trains each way, four to Springfield and two to Champaign. About noon on August 18, 1951, the 285 crossed the railroad tracks in Danville.

On April 20, 1952 cars 277 and 532 are caught by the author's Retina I camera negotiating a curve near Danville. Although the calendar says Spring is already one month old, Mother Nature has yet to provide leaves on the trees. About six months previous, the 277 had made one last trip through the Decatur shops receiving a modernized interior, indicating that the IT was still interested in its passenger business despite severely declining patronage numbers.

VERMILLION RIVER BRIDGE

This is obviously a "posed" shot. A two car westbound train sits atop the 1150 foot long bridge over the Vermilion River, west of Danville. The motorman, offended and disturbed by the delay occasioned by our impromptu photo stop, has an impatient stare on his face. The problem for we photographers was it was easier for us to get down to the river bed to take the shot than it was to climb back up to the train!

OPOSSUM TROT TRESTLE

The sun is on the north side of the Opossum Trot trestle as a two car train moves west. This trestle was at the bottom of a downgrade heading west from Danville and more or less represented a problem spot on the single track line. This trestle was one of the factors which contributed to the line being the first IT main line abandonment, on April 26, 1952. Eastbound trains henceforth turned at Watkins, Ill.

At this point we are treated to my all time favorite color photo taken of the "Traction". As is usually the case with a classic view, this shot was totally unrehearsed. It occurred as follows: While on an October 13, 1951 trip to Birmingham, Alabama, we were driving along the IT Danville line on what is now Illinois Rt. 150. *We heard the blast of an air horn so the 1950 Ford was halted. In a moment or so, the orange beauty of IT 263 appeared on Opossum Trot trestle. All the variables clicked, right opportunity, right sun, right time! Please enjoy!*

Whereas many of the cities IT served were bypassed, taking the cars off the streets, Danville was not. In early 1952, the city wanted to repave the main drag and eliminate the car tracks. The Danville to Springfield line was cut back to Watkins, Ill., on April 26, 1952 authorized by ICC Finance Docket 17337. This shortened *the line by about 15 miles. It was not long until another three mile "clipping" occurred cutting the line back to Ogden. In this September 9, 1951 shot, we see eastbound car 285 passing the Ogden waiting shelter. The cars still ran all the way to Danville at this time.*

OGDEN

Special train cars 274-531 turn on the Ogden wye for a return trip to Springfield following the line abandonment east towards Danville. Ogden was a hamlet incorporated in 1883 that did not live up to its founders' expectation, even though it was served by the NYC in addition to the IT. The Fielding Grain Co. Elevator, Standard Oil Co. and Hunter Lumber Company were located along the NYC. The IT also served the Hunter Lumber which was also a coal distributor in the days when most homes were heated by coal.

The May 29, 1955 two car special plugs along westbound from Ogden. Note the IT call box shelter used by the IT crews to converse with the dispatcher in the days before radios. The skies here indicate that it will possibly rain. Unfortunately for the cameramen, the prediction came true later in the trip.

16

GLOVER TOWER

We are looking south across the tracks of the Peoria and Eastern Railroad (a NYC subsidiary) at the Glover tower. The interchange at this location considerably benefited the IT as "The Traction" received some of its most lucrative revenue with the Chicago and Eastern Illinois R.R. traffic destined to points on the C&EI line as well as traffic destined off C&EI rails at Evansville, Indiana. The Champaign County Grain Association had an elevator at Glover, served exclusively by the IT.

An April 20, 1952 view of Glover Tower. This tower, in common with most interlocking towers, has been gone for many years.

Evidence of how busy Glover interchange must have been in earlier days is this shot of it taken from the adjacent highway bridge. The IT train is on the Danville-Springfield line. Curving off to the left is the connection with the C&EI. The single track to the right is the main line of the Peoria and Eastern, running from Peoria to Indianapolis by way of Danville. P&E offered two passenger trains a day over that route in the 1940s.

ST. JOSEPH

The distance from Glover to St. Joseph, Ill was a scant two miles. While the population of Glover was almost nil, St. Joseph had a population of 810 and boasted a brick combination passenger station-substation.

CHAMPAIGN

Champaign is a college town, home to the University of Illinois. Car 285 is seen here at Champaign on April 20, 1952. The IT is running over Wabash Railroad tracks at this location. In 1937 the IT abandoned the street trackage through town to relieve traffic congestion, and utilized the private right-of-way afforded by the Wabash. Both freight and passenger service was improved as a result.

18

A two-car westbound train is seen at the Champaign station. To the left of the train is the substantially built, tile roofed, P&E (NYC) passenger station. In 1952 Champaign had a population of about 23,000, far less than the present day.

The Illinois Terminal tended to assign certain cars to certain lines rather than have all cars roam all over the system. Car 285, a car regularly assigned to the Danville line prior to its abandonment in April, 1952, is running as Train #62 (Springfield-Danville). It is leaving Champaign station. The station bears both the Wabash and ITC names. This shot was one of my earliest color slides, taken on September 9, 1951.

TURNING THE CARS AROUND

Almost all of the Illinois Terminal's interurban cars were single ended by design. This required that there be either wyes or turning loops wherever a run terminated, for whatever reason. IT city, suburban and PCC cars were double ended. During the last few years of operation, the IT sometimes paired two single ended cars back to back, in order to avoid the problems of turning where there were no facilities. Car 203 is on the wye on Randolph Street, Champaign. By the time this view was taken on September 3, 1954, the line had been cut back to a new eastern terminal at Champaign. Car 203 was an ex-Bloomington line car #1203, having run most of its life on the Peoria-Bloomington-Decatur line. It was renumbered 203 in February, 1953.

Rather than turning on the wye as car 203 in the previous photo had done, 285 "loops" around the locomotive storage area for its return to Springfield. This was indeed an auspicious day, June 11, 1955, the last time a regularly scheduled IT passenger run would leave Champaign.

A true "one time" shot. At the Champaign station, we see 285 ready to depart for Springfield as Train #63. Its departure however, has been delayed by the appearance of an Illinois Central special train which is wying through the IT Champaign station. It is a football special from Chicago. At the time this photo was taken, 2:25 PM, the IT train is 15 minutes late in leaving. Since I rode that train I can vouch for the fact that it arrived in Decatur on time at 3:20 PM. It was the hottest ride I ever had on the IT, a road noted for its aggressive motormen.

Champaign freight house was a nice yellow brick structure, as this October 17, 1953 view will testify. It was built well, many said "for the ages", as were most of the ITS passenger and freight structures. Even 40-plus years later, many remain standing and used for purposes other than railroad use.

THE LAST TRAIN FROM CHAMPAIGN

A "Last Run" car is at Randolph Street in Champaign. Car 285 has completed the loop through the IT freight yard and is returning to the station to pick up the last passenger to ride an IT car out of Champaign. On this day, June 11, 1955, it is raining for the occasion.

If only crowds like this had boarded IT trains on other days, there probably would not have ever been a "Last Run." The mournful crowd surges aboard 285, creating a standing load as it leaves for the west. Most riders had purchased tickets only to the next station, Bondville, just so they could say they rode the last passenger run on the line.

BONDVILLE

In a photograph that rated a double page "spread" in TRAINS Magazine a few years ago, the last day car plods along a few miles west of Champaign. Soon it would cross Illinois Route 10 as it approached Bondville. The slow speed was occasioned by a cooperative motorman who did not want to arrive at the next station until the harried conductor had had a chance to collect all the cash fares of the many riders who were only riding the one station.

East of Bondville, on a happier and sun lit day, car 284 rushed west with train #3. The passengers on board could be counted on one hand, leading to the aforementioned un-happy last run.

Eastbound cars 274-531 move past the Bondville station and substation. Considering that the population of the town was a mere 44 souls, one might be tempted to say that the IT overbuilt there. I vividly recall making this shot, as the IT motorman, with no side vision of the road he was crossing, zipped thru the intersection at 60 mph!

OUTRUNNING AN INTERURBAN

Because of the slow pace of the last day train, one was able to out run it by automobile to Bondville. That is a feat that I was never able to duplicate when chasing a regular run over that course. IT took 12 minutes to cover that 7 mile distance. Problem was that if you took the road to go between the same points, the mileage was about 15, with a strong possibility of getting stuck behind a tractor hauling a load of hay.

The next station to the west of Bondville was Seymour (1940 population, 240). Seymour had first been served by the Illinois Central Railroad's Champaign to Havana branch, a 104 mile line that catered to its passengers by allowing its passenger tickets to be used on the interurban at commonly served towns along the line so that they could get off at intermediate stops closer to their destination. Industry there consisted of two grain elevator companies. Both were exclusively served by the IC. A lumber yard and a farm implement dealer were served by the interurban company.

WHITE HEATH

White Heath's brick passenger station is being passed by car 285 on the rainy last day of operation, June 11, 1955. This small town had long ago ceased being even a marginal contributor towards IT revenues.

The frame Illinois Central depot is the "attention getter" in this view. It is remarkable to consider that the small town of White Heath with a population of 350 at the time the photo was taken enjoyed passenger services from two railroads, IT and IC. All carload freight service to the town was rendered by the IC. This is whatever was delivered to the sole industry, the White Heath grain and Supply Company. Reflecting on this last day of passenger service, one wonders if the cost of constructing the brick IT station was ever recovered in revenues.

MONTICELLO

Monticello was the location of the infamous "S" curve that made it such a photogenic location to photograph the interurban cars. This photo, taken on September 3, 1954, shows one of the ubiquitous Railway Express trucks loading westbound car 203 at the station building.

The 203 works the classic yellow brick station at Monticello, a town of over 2,500 people. Oddly, the IT served only one industry at this location. The other 13 industries on the town had their freight car needs equally divided between the IC and the Wabash Railroads.

26

A three car ILLINI RAILROAD CLUB SPECIAL train pauses on the "S" curve at Monticello to let the fans take their photos of the train. The date is September 19, 1954, about nine months before passenger service would end there for all time, June 11, 1955.

Our last photo at Monticello is on the sad rain-filled June, 1955 last day of passenger operations. The atmospheric conditions matched the sadness of all who loved the IT interurbans.

27

BEMENT

Bement, 28 miles west of Champaign, was blessed with a brick IT station building and a population of 1,466. Some of the town folks got into special garb to greet the passage of their last passenger run. The station building also housed the manual substation owned by Illinois Power and Light Co. This "sub" could produce 2,000 amps of current for IT passenger and freight trains. A similar rectifier set in today's technology would be about the size of two soft drink dispensing machines.

In a shot that would have greatly benefited from a wide angle lens, a two car IT train charges down the main street of Cerro Gordo. The town, named after a famous battle in the Mexican War, boasted a large frame, one-story station. This was a case of the steam road (Wabash) serving a town having a passenger station at least the equal of its interurban competitor. The steam road, being there first, naturally had all of the industries in town on its line. The Harry J. Cox elevator was the only carload shipper located on IT iron. Photo taken May 29, 1952.

28

LAKE DECATUR

Just south of Decatur, the Sangamon River was dammed creating a large lake. This resulted in the IT building a lengthy span in order to cross the lake. If my memory serves me correctly, this lake had an inordinately large population of turtles that must have been periodically disturbed by the interurbans rumbling overhead.

When the *Streamliners* were placed in service, the trains were parked in major "on line" towns, so they could be inspected by the public. The initial reaction was positive, but short lived.

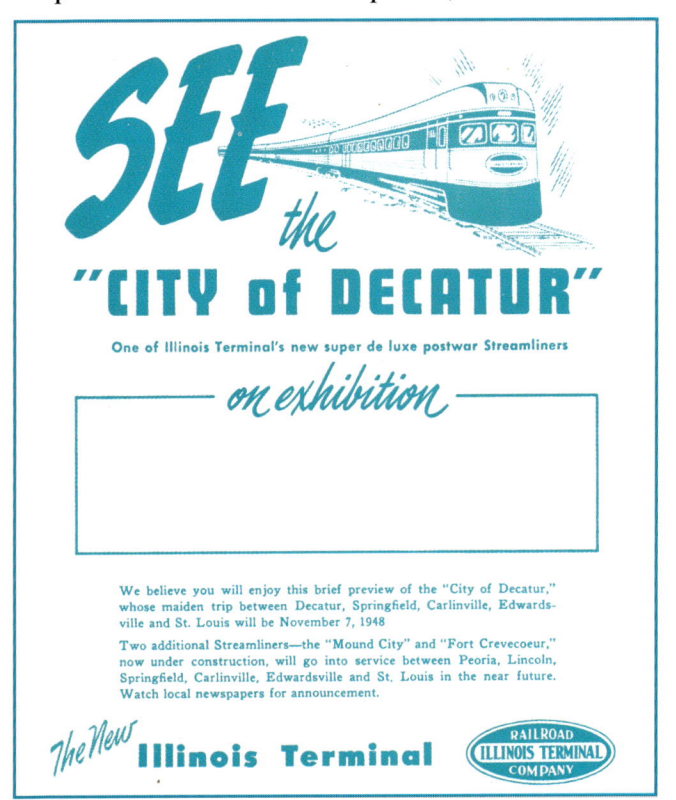

Painted in the classic "traction orange" livery, the way interurbans were meant to be, car 280 swings north onto the line to Peoria via Bloomington. Car 270, one of IT's two longest coaches, is moving westward from Danville to Springfield. Cars 270 and 271 were originally built as 68 foot long parlor cars in 1909 for the Columbus, Delaware & Marion, in Ohio, but were purchased by the IT at an early date. This location was the junction between the two lines. In the early days of the IT, the Decatur-Bloomington line was originally called the Chicago, Bloomington and Decatur. The promoters were indeed filled with optimism, but in those heady times, there was no limit to conjuring up names of destinations that could never be attained. In this case, only the Decatur-Bloomington part of the title was fulfilled. Photo taken, June 24, 1950.

SEE the "CITY of DECATUR"
One of Illinois Terminal's new super de luxe postwar Streamliners
— on exhibition —

We believe you will enjoy this brief preview of the "City of Decatur," whose maiden trip between Decatur, Springfield, Carlinville, Edwardsville and St. Louis will be November 7, 1948

Two additional Streamliners—the "Mound City" and "Fort Crevecoeur," now under construction, will go into service between Peoria, Lincoln, Springfield, Carlinville, Edwardsville and St. Louis in the near future. Watch local newspapers for announcement.

The New Illinois Terminal   ILLINOIS TERMINAL RAILROAD COMPANY

DECATUR

On October 17, 1953, car 285 paused at the new (in 1931) Decatur station on an afternoon run to Springfield. Those were glorious days, especially in the Fall, when the mid-day light was relatively low and many fans were of the opinion that the Illinois Terminal would live forever.

One wonders if the patrons at the Van Dyke Grill appreciated the fact that this would be the last time that they would see an IT passenger car at the Decatur station. Probably not, as the world was moving too fast, and if there was discussion about transport matters at the tables, it was more likely about Fords and Chevys, rather than about interurban cars built in 1914 by St. Louis Car Co.

In a shot taken from the adjacent Wabash Railroad bridge, car 285 moves towards Springfield. The rain made photography difficult and the geometry between the location of the bridge and the IT track added another impediment to the composition of this view. Oh well, it cannot be taken any more so a half a loaf is better than no bread at all.

After passenger service was abandoned, freight continued, often powered by the distinctive Class "D" streamlined locomotives. Here we see #71 coming westward under the same Wabash Railroad bridge at Decatur.

ELECTRIFIED FREIGHT

In the days before "automatic film advance" was available on cameras, it was not easy to get more than one shot of a moving train at any given place. This September 3, 1955 shot was taken a few seconds after the preceding view of #71. These workhorse locomotives had been downgraded from Peoria St. Louis service to work on the Springfield-Danville line (or rather, what remained of it). Diesels had already taken over freight work on the main line.

Moving through a park west of Decatur, 71 is beginning to pick up speed with its train. These locomotives were built at the IT's Decatur Shops during 1940 to 1942. Specifically, 71 was built using parts from Class "C" unit 1581 and tipped the scales at a whopping 217,000 pounds.

Coming "up for air" after dipping under the Illinois Central Railroad's original Cairo-Freeport main line, IT 273 heads for Decatur in this September 9, 1951 view. Today, not only is the IT line gone, but likewise most of the IC trackage through the center of Illinois.

32

HARRISTOWN

Harristown, with a population of only 150, had this massive yellow (buff) brick station to serve its passenger and express needs. "Express", to the IT, was in large part, daily shipments of milk from farm to city coupled with the return flow of empty cans. Built in the halcyon days of the century's first decade, the station epitomized the optimism of the time Bill Middleton referred to as the "Interurban Era".

A two-car special hurtles past the Harristown station on May 29, 1955, about two weeks before the end of service over the line. This station also housed the semi-automatic 2,000 amp substation, thus this train had plenty of power on its westward flight.

33

On the west side of Harristown, class "D" motor 71 plods east with a local freight. My friend, Don Idarious and I spent a wonderful morning chasing this local, starting near Springfield and following it as far as Decatur. The Wabash station for Harristown can seen at the right. Quite a comedown compared to the station that the IT offered the town.

NIANTIC

Even closer to Springfield on an early September day in 1955, locomotive 71 passes the Wabash station at Niantic. Niantic is four miles west of Harristown and boasted a population 5 times that of Harristown. Oddly though, the IT had seen fit to construct only a one-story hip-roofed frame station at Niantic, similar to that of the Wabash (as seen to the right) at that location. Niantic had the usual grain elevator (Niantic Farmers Grain Co.) which was, of course served by the WAB. Two other carload users in the town could be handled by the IT.

ILLIOPOLIS

Often a sign tells the story of a town in a quite dramatic manner. This sign gives Illiopolis some good press. It would have been marvelous if I could have shot the sign with an IT train in the view, but it was located on the north side of the road, while the IT, at this point was south of the road. Spring was indeed in the air on this late winter's day, March 12, 1955.

Not without thy wondrous story,
Illinois, Illinois,
Can be writ the nation's glory,
Illinois, Illinois,
On the record of thy years
Abraham Lincoln's name appears,
Grant and Logan, and our tears,
Illinois.

The brick station at Illiopolis greets the arrival of train 62 on July 17, 1954, running from Springfield to Decatur. Down the street, to the west, is the Illiopolis Grain Co. elevator.

At the same location, but after passenger service had been terminated, locomotive 71 and its train pass the Illiopolis station. The station, 22 miles west of Springfield, also housed a substation. Curiously the building survives to this day (1998). This view was taken on a cloudless September 3, 1955.

Locomotive 71 glides along what is now Illinois Rt. 631, west of Illiopolis, on October 17, 1953. This indeed "Corn Country" as the harvested stalks to the right will testify. Illiopolis, in 1947 had a population of 714 and was served by the Wabash RR as well as the IT. Further evidence of its sophisticaton was that it had a movie theater, the Illiopolis Theater, which could seat 300, almost half the town's population.

A troublesome grade crossing was eliminated by construction of this fine bridge over what is now Rt. 631. On May 29, 1955 we caught 274-531 as they raced across the highway. The weather could have been better!

On a sunnier day, September 3, 1955, about three months after the previous shot of the passenger train moving west, we see a freight crossing the same IT bridge with a sizable train. It was in this general area, that a large munitions complex was built in 1942. The Sangamon Ordinance Plant was served by both the IT and Wabash and shipped thousands of carloads of the "stuff" of war to the US forces all over the world.

MECHANICSBURG BRANCH

Mechanicsburg is one of those tiny rural towns that tend to exist, though the original reason for their creation can only be speculated. The hamlet, (423 people in 1947) was bypassed by the Wabash Railroad when it was built from Decatur to Springfield and beyond to the Mississippi River. The town folk sought to remedy being left "High and Dry" by constructing a horse car line about 3 miles long from Buffalo to the town. Then came the Traction in the early 1900s and it too built west, missing Mechanicsburg. The almost 20 years of horse operation of the branch had been demonstrated to be inadequate and the IT was persuaded to build a branch about two miles long to the hamlet in 1905. This scene of a two-car special train at the "cut-back" end of the branch some 50 years later, was a great event. The train rests at Mechanicsburg Grain Elevator Co. We hasten to add that the dirt road in the photo is not the highway connection to town. There was a paved road along the tree line.

The visit by the special train to Mechanicsburg was over and the train climbed out of the low spot marking the location of the town. As I recall, the voltage was so low at the grain elevator, which was then the end of the branch, that the passengers had to get off the car so it could get the "strength" to climb back up to the main line. This was difficult to understand, as there was a 2,000 amp manual substation at Buffalo, only a few miles distant. Probably poor rail bonding was the source of the problem. The straight track is the main line, looking east.

38

BUFFALO IN 1984

Tracks and wire of the Illinois Terminal no longer run in front of the buff passenger/substation at Buffalo. They were ripped out shortly after the official abandonment of the line, December 1, 1959. The date is July 18, 1984, and the electrified line to Danville has been gone to the Trolley Valhalla (that must exist somewhere) for almost 30 years. Buildings built as sound as this were just too good to rate the wrecking ball. They will probably still be around in the 21st Century.

DAWSON

After a chase, in which I got my 1951 Ford up to about 80 mph, I finally caught car 263 in a hastily framed shot heading west at Dawson, a place 10 miles east of Springfield and 111 miles from Danville. No, the Dawson Grain Co. elevator is not located on the IT. One can note that the Wabash had the set of tracks that served it. This photo was taken on one of those splendid Fall days (September 29, 1951) that are par for central Illinois.

RIVERTON

Down the gravel street in Riverton, the white flagged special train moves west towards Springfield, a scant 6 miles distant. Weather could have been better, but as the saying goes, "You just can't take shots like this today."

In the waning days of winter, (March 12, 1955) orange car 263 sped east, crossing the Sangamon River. To the literary minded, *the famous "Spoon River" tales, written by Edgar Lee Masters, used this area as the basis for the stories.*

End of the line, at least the 121 mile Danville to Springfield line was this location. On the "back side" of the station we see a variety of IT cars including an "abbreviated" Streamliner. *The* Streamliner *parlor car at the far right is the LOUIS JOLIET (car 350), out of service when this view was taken on April 16, 1955.*

PEORIA-SPRINGFIELD-ST. LOUIS MAIN LINE

The Illinois Terminal Railroad Main Line consisted of 75 miles of single track extending from Peoria to Springfield and an additional 100 miles from Springfield to St. Louis. Service began over the route in 1910, after the McKinley bridge was completed over the Mississippi, and continued until the abandonment of passenger service on June 11, 1955. Freight service continued to be offered, only by trackage rights agreements over paralleling railroads, that changed ownership every couple of years.

The route was famous for the upgraded passenger service offered beginning in 1949 with the delivery of three *Streamliner* trains sets built by St. Louis Car Company. One of the sets turned off the main line at Springfield and operated east as far as Decatur.

The new equipment failed to stem the depleting tide of passengers and gradually the *Streamliner* services were withdrawn. The last passenger train from Springfield to St. Louis operated March 3, 1956.

SPRINGFIELD

One of the "Crown Jewels" of IT station buildings was the building on Clear Lake Road in Springfield. It was opened in 1933. A just-arrived Streamliner *pokes its nose into the photo at the left, September 3, 1955. Other notable IT passenger stations were those at Peoria and the monumental St. Louis, MO edifice, sort of the jewel at the top to the crown.*

In my memory, the Illinois Terminal was the electric line with the big orange cars, unadorned but for the legend "Illinois Terminal" on the letterboard, and the distinctive oval on the car side bearing the identical legend. Simple, distinctive, and memorable. Everything that was necessary to identify the car, the owning company, and to create within the potential rider the thought that here was a solid dependable and safe means of travel.

42

Another method of sending the IT message was to provide a map of the system, showing that it was a part of the history of the Prairie State, in addition to being an essential link in the commerce of that state. The main lines of the TRACTION are shown, as well as the so-called Valley Division, which ran from Joliet west to Princeton, following the Illinois River valley. The artist has shown some imagination in indicating that the Valley Division also served Chicago, a dream that never did materialize.

Another example of advertising material is the IT hand out of the "Measure Service". Liberally distributed, it is an example of "spreading the word".

43

EAST PEORIA

On a Fall day in 1955, line car 1705 and Class B locomotive 1569, painted in an unusual green paint scheme for that class stand in front of the East Peoria terminal building. E. Peoria rather than Peoria became the northern terminus of the IT in 1950. The trackage over the river was abandoned because of a combination of high bridge maintenance and clearance problems with the new Streamliners *on the Peoria side of the river.*

A three-car "Blue Train" (i.e. one that included a parlor-diner) is being substituted for the ailing Streamliner Fort Crevecoeur *on May 13, 1950 at East Peoria. The* Streamliners *were very trouble prone in their early years and the old standard cars soldiered on.*

44

In front of the new shop at East Peoria, a three-car train is held in reserve awaiting a call to duty when one of the Streamliners *called in sick.*

This view of the newly constructed shop in East Peoria indicates that the scope of repair ability was quite extensive. To the right in the photo can be seen two sheet metal buildings that made up the temporary East Peoria station in this early 1950 view. Buses brought passengers over from Peoria, an operation that seemed to give little inconvenience.

PEORIA-E. PEORIA SHUTTLE

In 1949, after the Streamliners *proved to be incapable of entering and leaving the Peoria station, a shuttle car service was instituted between the station and a new terminal completed in East Peoria. Center-entrance cars and ex-Valley Division suburban cars were rotated in to shuttle passengers across the Illinois River until such time as permission was granted to abandon the bridge and track. The shuttle operation was finally abandoned on June 8, 1950. On May 13, 1950, about three weeks before line over the bridge was abandoned, shuttle car 410 crosses.*

MACKINAW JUNCTION

Sixteen miles down the line from East Peoria was Mackinaw Junction Tower. At this location, the Bloomington line separated from the main line. The main went on south to Springfield and St. Louis while the Bloomington line went easterly to Bloomington and then south to Decatur via Clinton. The photo was taken in 1950 by my friend Eugene Van Dusen.
(Eugene Van Dusen, Gordon Lloyd Collection)

46

The buff colored brick passenger station/substation at Mackinaw Junction remains a National Historic Site. Freight trains still rumbled by on the other side of the station when this photo was taken in 1981. The line had been regraded and relocated off the former electrified trackage using former Pennsylvania Railroad trackage. The branch to Bloomington had been gone for 28 years. The substation formerly located in the building was a manually operated 3,000 amp affair.

At Panther Creek, south of Mackinaw on September 19, 1981, a diesel freight powered by a GP38-2 (acquired after the IT was taken over by the N&W) leads the train headed for Springfield. **(Kevin Idarius, Gordon Lloyd Collection)**

The same train passes Minier, a junction point between the N&W and the ICG at the time the photo was taken. **(Kevin Idarius, Gordon Lloyd Collection)**

LINCOLN

Lincoln was about midway between E. Peoria and Springfield. A southbound *Streamliner* crosses the Gulf, Mobile & Ohio tracks just north of town. The IT being the junior line was obligated to staff the tower. The date is March 12, 1955 only a month before service ended over the line.

Two years after the end of electrified service, the Lincoln freight house and adjacent storage yard appeared desolate. In the yard, cars 096 and 203 quietly await the scrapper. Car 096 was originally motor car 249, built by American Car and Foundry in 1908. In 1944 it was converted to a caboose numbered 990 and then in 1947, it was made into a bunk car and renumbered 096. It was finally put out of its misery in 1962.

49

When declining passenger business dictated a reduction in Streamliner train size, the IT responded by cutting the train size from two cars to one. This, of course, destroyed all sense of aesthetics for the train, found here on the Main Line near Lincoln.

The April 27, 1952 time table is not as lavish as the one issued in 1949. The line from Danville has been cut back to Watkins, IL and the number of daily trains reduced to three. Similar "chopping" is evidenced on the Bloominton-Decatur-Springfield route, now down to four trains a day. A double page is devoted to ITC freight service, showing a change in emphasis toward freight-only operation.

SHERMAN

Near Sherman, a southbound diesel powered freight prepares to cross the Sangamon River. The two GP-s powering the train were purchased in 1953. These locomotives produced 1,500 HP each, where a single Class "D" was rated at the equivalent of 1,800 horsepower. When the Class "D"s were in the vicinity of a substation, they had greater capability then when at a distance from same. Electric locomotives had an advantage of not having to generate their own electricity. This feature of course proved to be their ultimate downfall because the Geeps could generate their own electricity irrespective of their nearness to a substation.

Car 301 moves south towards Sherman, a small town of 250, about 6.4 miles north of Springfield. Photo was taken in 1955.

PARLOR CAR SERVICE

North of Springfield, as I was riding in the parlor car of the southbound FORT CREVE COEUR, we encountered a meet with the northbound MOUND CITY. This was one of the high points of the IT passenger operation, new trains equipped with the best, having amenities equal to that found on the GM&O's ANN RUTTLEGE. The two-car MOUND CITY speeds north, having left Springfield at 12:13 PM. It will arrive at E. Peoria at 1:55 PM, this June 30, 1951. Parlor car operation ceased over this route exactly three months later, September 30th.

Nearing Springfield, single car 301 swings into a gentle curve on an early Spring day in 1955. The Streamliners *had gone from three-car trains, when built in 1949, to two car trains in 1951 down to singles at the end of service.*

An Illinois Central 0-6-0 is producing a lot of smoke as it shuttles back and forth drilling freight cars near the Pillsbury Mills elevators in Springfield. Placidly awaiting the next run is 1200 with an ex-C&LE trailer car in the 600-series tacked on behind. It is interesting to consider that the 1200 was originally built as an express motor car by Mc Guire Cummings in 1910. As built, it only had 20 seats, in the rear of the car. In 1920, the 1200s were rebuilt as standard combines having 50 seats. This photo was taken June 24, 1950, not long before the car was involved in a crossing accident and scrapped.

SPRINGFIELD

A two-car Streamliner backs into the Springfield station in July, 1954. This train does not have a parlor car since that service had been dropped almost three years previous. That action marked the beginning of the end for IT passenger service.

On July 27, 1954 car 274 is seen sitting over the inspection pit at Springfield, while on adjacent track a fully inspected car is ready to roll back into service.

Behind the Springfield terminal are 274 and 531. Car 531 was a motorized trailer with two traction motors. It had received air-conditioning in 1937 and was sold for scrap in 1956. In this May 23, 1955 scene, they are awaiting yet another run to either St. Louis or E. Peoria.

53

Diesels had been a mainstay on the IT for over a quarter century when this shot of 1504 was taken at Springfield on June 15, 1977. The train, consisting of covered hoppers is seen stretching to the viewing limit. The 1504 was purchased in 1953, after the IT passed from local control to a consortium of Class I railroads.

A bit south of the Springfield passenger station, we find a Class "B" locomotive switching in a freight yard as the sun sinks into the west. 1566 was built in 1910 in the Decatur Shop. In 1952 it was sold to the Illinois Power and Light at Danville for use in switching hopper cars. Photo taken on September 27, 1951.

"MINI-STREAMLINERS"

Leaving the Springfield station, single car 301 curves around the freight facility southbound heading for St. Louis. Class "B", "C", and "D" locomotives are seen on September 3, 1955 in the background, while the main line of the GM&O is to the left.

The awkward look of a single car Streamliner is emphasized in this shot taken in Springfield in April, 1955. Downsizing, a word not used in the 1950s is indeed portrayed in this scene.

Liquor, beer and gasoline signs frame the 301 as she leaves Springfield for Missouri's premier city. Although it was reduced to a single car train, the ride was still wonderful and the Traction was doing its best!

THE END OF THE LINE HAS BEEN REACHED

Wearing black, the color signifying a state of mourning, the last fantrip on the St. Louis-Springfield line moves north on March 3, 1956. Cars 284-530-531 make up the cortege.

Not the best of my IT views, this shot nevertheless has historic value. The last passenger run from St. Louis has tied up at Springfield. The two-car Streamliner train represented the end of IT inter-city passenger service. The date, March 3, 1956.

CHATHAM

Chatham sees the passage of a southbound train comprised of 276-531 on September 29, 1951. The men seen boarding the train are all "deadheads", i.e. IT employees who are riding on passes to an assignment in the St. Louis area.

Class "C" 1590 with a train composed primarily of tank cars, is seen moving south from Chatham, 11 miles south of Springfield, on August 7, 1954. Three of the other locomotives in the class were stripped and upgraded to Class "D" prior to World War II, but the program was not resumed after the War. Instead, diesels were bought.

57

VIRDEN

Riding in the motorman's cab on car 301 entering Virden, we can look down the main drag. It is the last day of passenger operation, March 3, 1956, and this will be the very last southbound passenger run. History in the making.

The initial enthusiasm created by the *Streamliners*, made mention of them prime elements in advertising. Illinois citizens were longing for new transportation facilities. In the case of the *Streamliners* the IT management was truly proud of their new trains and used that positive view in their ads.

The CB&Q crossing at Virden, population 3,000, in 1947, located in Macoupin County. The IT had no track connection with the two steam roads serving the town, the CB&Q and the GM&O.

Dwight Pittman (coal and ice) was the only one of Virden's eight carload receivers served by the IT.

Trouble has surfaced at Anderson Substation, Milepost 109 (from Peoria). It is the last day of service, and the regular train has lost its trolley shoe. The motorman and conductor are fitting a new one on car 301. One of the sources of its problems looms in the background!

This 1950 calendar was a low-cost method of advertising the Illinois Terminal. In 1950, there was still an element of faith that the *Streamliners* would prevail and return riders to IT rails. The million dollar investment in passenger equipment was doomed to failure, as the American "love affair" with their automobiles was an irreversable trend. Good try Illinois Terminal.

59

GIRARD

Curious inhabitants of Girard are at the station as the agent interrogates the motorman. He is probably explaining the late arrival of his train due to the lost trolley shoe at Anderson "sub". The usual buff-colored IT station is at the right. Girard was quite a railroad center. The GM&O, CB&Q, and C&NW all served the town in addition to the IT.

May 15, 1989, some 24 years after the 301 and its companion car stopped for the last regular southbound passenger run. The Girard station is shown serving as a private residence. The building, too good to tear down, is now a cozy home for a family, who we can only hope, appreciates its heritage.

GILLESPIE

Entering Gillespie from the north, Car 301 leaves the private right-of-way and enters Elm Street. Gillespie was a medium sized town with a population of about 4,500. The town had four carload industries, two located on the New York Central. The other two were served by the IT. They were the quaintly named "Little Dog Coal Company" and the prosaic "Jack Young Company" (coal, sand, and gravel).

Cruising down Gillespie's main drag, 301 moves south. From the railfan seat, on the left side of the car a couple of young fans view the passing scene.

A four-car "extra" moves north through Gillespie, on September 19, 1954.

BENLD

The IT station at Benld was three miles, by rail, from Gillespie. Whereas the population in 1947 was about 2,500, today it numbers only about 1,500. One could draw a conclusion that the loss of the interurban made the town a less desirable place to live. Another point of view would be that the population loss of the small towns along the line was one of the reasons that the IT is no longer with us. Note the unique train order signals located adjacent to the station.

STAUNTON

A red brick station building served as the IT stop in Staunton, (1947 population 4,212). An interesting feature of the station was the second floor dispatcher's office, graced by a bay window. Staunton had grown a bit to the point where now it had 4,744 residents. It once was served not only by the IT, but also by the Litchfield and Madison Railway and the Wabash Railroad (referred to by some as the "W.A.Bash Company!"). The L&M later became a branch of the C&NW.

63

The "Last Day" funeral train can be noted at Staunton on March 3, 1956. Staunton was the junction point with a branch line that proceeded northeasterly to Litchfield and Hillsboro. There were three passenger round trips on that branch each day in 1930. The 8.9 mile Hillsboro-Litchfield line was abandoned in 1933. The line from Staunton to Litchfield was gone a few years before WW II began in Europe.

The shot I took of 302 at Hamel should have been in a vertical format, but the train was approaching so fast that good photo composition was not possible. This hamlet had a population of 128 on April 16, 1955, the date this photo was made. It has now grown to about 550 despite the fact that it has no rail service whatsoever.

64

EDWARDSVILLE

In Edwardsville two IT Geep locos power a freight train over trackage that was once electrified and routinely witnessed the passage of Class "D" freight locomotives. With over 8,000 people, the town was the County Seat of Madison County.

The motorman having left the cab of the Streamliner at the Edwardsville station, had left the hinged cab door open. A conference with the agent was in progress. The attractive red brick station was opened to the public in late 1938. On that same date, street running in Edwardsville came to an end, to the jubilation of the freight crews.

GRANITE CITY

Peoria was not the only place that presented operational problems for the Streamliners. Street running in Granite city entailed sharp curves that were impossible for the Streamliners to negotiate. Therefore, the rather splendid two-story brick station in downtown was shuttered, and passenger service moved to the belt line around Granite City. The small sheet metal building to the left served until the last day of passenger service, March 3, 1956, the date this photo was taken.

Operating between Granite City and St. Louis, the last day "Railfan Special" crosses over the rail yards at Venice. Just prior to crossing the Mississippi River on the high McKinley Bridge.

Following the last day special passenger train is a local freight powered by an Alco model S-2, built in 1948. The 1000 HP work horse had zebra stripes painted across its ends in order to help avoid grade crossing accidents. This shot in brilliant sunshine on March 3, 1956 helps put a happy face on an otherwise sad day in IT history.

ST. LOUIS TERMINAL

Yes, this is a posed shot. One might imagine that making a photo of any piece of IT equipment with a St. Louis Public Service (SLPS) PCC in the same view would be easy. Not so! A view of the two companies' equipment in one photo took over 1 1/4 hours of patient waiting. It was worth the wait though, as 40 years later SLPS ("SLOPS") 1662 and IT 458 have gone to the never-never land of trolley cars. The SLPS car was operating on the Broadway line, a line that was abandoned August 20, 1956, almost two years prior to the demise of the IT Granite City car line.

On a cloudy day, at the same location as the preceding photograph, we find IT 276 heading for Peoria on a mid-day run. During the latter years, IT ran only four daily passenger trains between St. Louis and Peoria.

67

THE ST. LOUIS ELEVATED STRUCTURE

Up on the elevated structure on July 1, 1951, we see 263 towing an express trailer number 603, one of a group of three ex-C&LE cars, bound for the St Louis terminal. The SLPS Broadway car line is just below.

A St. Louis-Alton center-entrance car is seen from the Broadway station of the IT. These were indeed "fast runners". A ride to Alton in the railfan seat of one of these cars was one of the "thrill" rides of the IT experience. Photo date, July 1, 1951. Alton suburban service via Granite City was discontinued on May 23, 1953. The cars soldiered on until 1958 serving Granite City commuters.

Unexpected visitors were continually showing up on the elevated structure. On June 7, 1952, IT 51, a combination trolley/battery/diesel locomotive (when it was built) nearly got me at Broadway station. I ran up to the platform and was able to get this "going away" shot of her. This unique locomotive was built by the St. Louis Car Company in 1930 as a demonstrator. In 1940, the batteries were removed, but its 300 HP Buda diesel still gave it freedom to roam away from the trolley wires.

REQUIEM FOR A LIGHTWEIGHT

My oldest son, Gordon, Jr. recorded this somber scene in St. Louis on a cold, dismal day, January 24, 1977. Sitting in a junk yard are the hulks of some of the IT Streamliners that had been introduced in 1949 with such hope and fanfare. If only they could have fulfilled the hopes and dreams of the late 1940's IT management.

THE ST. LOUIS SUBWAY

Fortunately the turning track on the ground floor (i.e. the basement) of the IT St. Louis station did allow adequate clearance for the Streamliners. *301 is shown on June 30, 1951 turning around for its trip back to Peoria. The St. Louis Statler Hotel in the background brings back memories of the many business trips I made to St. Louis to discuss railroad freight rate matters with the Missouri Pacific and Frisco. Passengers were required to either ride in a huge elevator or walk down three flights of steps to reach the trains from the waiting room.*

At the entrance to the IT subway leading to the St. Louis station, the engineer has the controller on the last notch as he blasts up the grade with a short train in the Fall of 1954. This was many years before the landmark Gateway Arch was built.

IT Streamliner *301 is exiting the St. Louis subterranean terminal, this time with train #96, scheduled to arrive in Decatur at 8:40 PM on the evening of July 1, 1951.*

THE ST. LOUIS STATION

This neon sign outside the IT St. Louis station at 710 N. 12th Boulevard showed the extent of IT service. The extensive freight only trackage in and about St. Louis, in both Missouri and Illinois is disproportionately enlarged in this sign. But it did illustrate the IT running to Danville and Peoria, minus the Hillsboro line. I often wonder, if any fan got his hands on that sign for his private IT collection.

One would need a wide angle lens of epic proportions to take a shot of the entire IT St. Louis Terminal building which was 120 feet high. it was named the Midwest Terminal Building when completed in 1932. The presence of the Illinois Terminal in St. Louis was great.

71

PEORIA-BLOOMINGTON-DECATUR LINE

Unlike the other Illinois Terminal routes, the route from Peoria to Decatur, 83 miles, had very few on-line freight industries. Through service was begun in 1906 and was abandoned completely on February 21, 1953 with the exception of a short shuttle operation north out of Decatur 6 miles to Forsythe. This operation only lasted about two months.

Decatur was also home to the system backshops where the IT continued to refurbish and modernize its almost 40 year old rolling stock as late as 1953. The bulk of the passenger service was performed by a small group of combines, numbered 1200-1203. The sharp city street curves in downtown Bloomington offered railfans some extremely interesting operation.

The Staunton-Hillsboro line has been abbreviated to Litchfield, the route Danville-Ridge Farm is gone. Most drastic service cuts are on the "old line" Peoria-Bloomington-Decatur route which had shrunk to 7 R/T a day from the 10 R/T run offered twelve years earlier. In the schedule is a Peoria-Bloomington-Chicago schedule in connection with the Alton (GM&O) Bloomington to Chicago. This service competed with the direct Peoria-Chicago, CRI&P service of three hours, the IT-Alton service took seven hours. IT also advertised its 1 cent a mile R/T tickets good Fri-Sat-Sun. These tickets were favorites of University of Illinois students going home for the weekend.

CLINTON

My slide collection of the Mackinaw Junction to Decatur line via Bloomington is small. Most of my photos of this particular line are in black and white. The view above was taken as car 1202 stopped at the Clinton station. The brick station can be seen to the right, as can the wye which allowed the single end IT passenger cars to turn at the station. Clinton had a population of 6,300 in 1947 and was served by the Illinois Central R.R. in addition to the IT. most of the carload receivers were on the IC, but IT did serve the Illinois Power Company with fuel oil. Other IT-served businesses were the T.E. O'Brien Co. (sand, gravel, and cement) and Wade and Phillips (coal and oil).

MAROA

The IT station at Maroa was 9 miles south of Clinton. This photo was taken there on July 18, 1975. On February 21, 1953, the line was abandoned from Mackinaw Junction to Forsythe, 59.7 miles. This left P&E Farms and R.M. Penney, the line's only two industries "high and dry." Two customers in 60 miles was definitely not on a par with the other ITS routes, hence the reason for the track severance in February, 1953. After the route was abandoned, IT diesel freights operated between Peoria and Maroa over the Pennsy's Terre-Haute to Peoria secondary. Conrail ultimately abandoned this line also.

FORSYTHE

Cars 274 and 531 pose on a fantrip on the main street of Forsythe on May 29, 1955, a little over two years after the line north of the town was abandoned. The local population was unimpressed, as they had forsaken the IT trains many years ago.

73

An odd operation was the run of a shuttle car from Forsythe to Decatur, about 6 miles for a few more months after the line up to Bloomington was abandoned. Car 405, originally Chicago and Illinois Valley 61, was given ITS number 405 in 1930. This car, built in 1924, by St. Louis Car Co., was scrapped in 1956. Photo was taken on March 22, 1953, one month after the demise of the Decatur to Peoria via Bloomington service.

ALTON LINE

The operation from St. Louis to Alton, and then on to Grafton were rail routes distinctly and totally different in concept, and operation from the other "workings" of the Illinois Traction System. As a matter of record, the IT did not take over the operation of the so-called "Alton Line" until July 1, 1930. Consequently, no continuity of equipment, design, or practice existed between these distinct operations. Car 104, shown July 1, 1951 at Nameoki bears little or no resemblance to the main IT passenger fleet. The 104 was northbound waiting for a meet with a southbound run headed to St. Louis.

Car 100 is at Alton on June 6, 1952. The small center door inhibited fast loading and unloading of the car, but the high speed capability of the car made up for the seconds lost in the boarding and alighting process.

Car 123, built by the East St. Louis and Suburban Railway in 1924 is seen at the end of the line in Alton. This center-entrance car had double doors for faster loading and unloading of passengers. This improvement did not save the service from abandonment on March 7, 1953. This was a loss that, although lamented, deprived rapid access to St. Louis for the good people of Alton.

Later on at Nameoki, we witness a two car train of center entrance cars, 102 and 104 waiting for the St. Louis bound ALTON LIMITED. These cars were indeed tailor made for fast schedules between St. Louis and Alton. Built in 1917 by the American Car Co. (St. Charles, MO) they were very fast, and were really fun to ride.

WOOD RIVER

At Wood River, looking out the front of car 104 we note the passage of CB&Q train #43, the MARK TWAIN ZEPHYR, a run that traveled from St. Louis to Burlington, IA. This scene was taken on July 1, 1951.

GRAFTON LINE

North of Alton, the line to Grafton, about 15 miles, was not a rapid ride. The IT took over operation of the line in 1940. The line was always marginal and was operated with rail buses after their diminutive steam locomotive was scrapped. In this view, taken May 15, 1989, we see one of the ACF buses that operated on the line, now preserved at the Museum of Transportation in Barrett, MO.

On a happier day, June 8, 1952, 1939 White railbus 206 is in operation between Alton and Grafton, IL. This view taken out of the front window of 206 shows the muddy Mississippi. Even though it was a White railbus, it was powered by a Mack engine.

77

Two views of 206 being turned on the "Armstrong" turntable at Grafton. This rail-bus departed Alton for Grafton and intermediate stations at 6:15 AM, 8:30 AM, and 3:10 PM daily. Always a marginal operation, it is difficult to imagine that until 1933, the passenger service was handled by a steam locomotive hauling but one coach. The line was abandoned on May 23, 1953, thereby deleting 14.9 miles of very worn trackage from the IT inventory.

In reviewing the IT slides for this book, the thought has often recurred, what do the places look like today? There are some post abandonment views in this volume, but one that intrigues me the most regards the fate of the board and batten station at Grafton. In this shot taken on June 8, 1952, car (bus) 206 sits next to it waiting for its 4:25 PM departure to Alton. Could this building still be with us in 1998, some 46 years later? Since Grafton is so remote, I will probably never know.

78

ROSTER SHOTS

A property with the long life of the Traction, had dozens of main line passenger cars during its over 55 year existence. Color film was first introduced in the late 1930s but in the view of many, it and the cameras that used it, were not truly reliable until the late 1940s. In any event, the author did not begin color photography until May of 1950. Therefore, most of the color work in this volume dates from then.

Car 202, which had been 1202 until December 28, 1953, was built by Mc Guire Cummings (Paris, IL) in 1910. It was 45 years old when this portrait was taken. Cars 1202 and 1203 were renumbered 202-203 to make room for some leased flat cars on the roster in 1953.

IT 234 was built by Danville Car Co. in 1910. It was used as a business car on the IT and sold to the Illini Railroad Club in 1956. Although standing on IT tracks at Champaign in this March 23, 1957 view, it was not Illinois Terminal property. Fortunately this car is now at the Illinois Railway Museum at Union, IL, a place where it continues to receive loving care.

Not in first-class shape, but displaying its classic car architecture, 249 is an American Car and Foundry product of 1908. The date is June 24, 1950, one of my earliest color shots. Those leaded glass arches over the windows provide a splendor that reeks of the 1905 period. After a rest of a few months at Decatur, the car would be sold to Hyman-Michaels for scrap.

79

Here is one of the survivors of the IT, Illinois Valley Division, otherwise known as the Chicago, Ottawa, and Peoria, a dream that never became fulfilled. Car 263 was a regular on the Springfield-Danville line. She was built by Danville Car Co. in 1911 and shown at Springfield, on June 24, 1950.

273, built by the St. Louis Car Company in 1913, was 57'4" in length, and was powered by four GE 222G traction motors. In the March 12, 1955 afternoon sun at the Champaign station, she is "ready to fly" to Springfield. By this time, Champaign only saw one round trip per day.

Resting at Springfield after a fast run from St. Louis, car 276 (St. Louis, 1913) is "waiting for the beer." Yes, literally. A group of gregarious salesmen had asked the conductor if they could buy a couple of cases of beer and a tub filled with ice so as to have a party on the way to a Peoria sales affair. The "brains" said sure, but keep the tub and contents up in the baggage compartment. As a rider on this car, I was allowed to partake of their hospitality. You see, the IT served to please.

On October 17, 1953, we are back at the Decatur Shops of the IT to photograph car 278 (St. Louis, 1913). Although it is still in orange paint, it had been one of the first cars to be converted to air-conditioning. Air conditioning was introduced on the IT as early as 1927. The car was sold for scrap in May, 1954, about seven months after this photo was taken.

Last to be built of the conventional main-line passenger cars was IT 285. St. Louis Car Co. turned out this interurban classic in 1914, making her 41 years old at the time this photo was taken. Being the newest of IT cars, it was equipped with parlor seating and selected for service as the "Tangerine Flyer", in 1924. In 1928, however, the parlor seats were removed and the car was returned to regular coach/combine status. IT apparently preferred their parlor cars to be of the non-controlled variety. The 285 was scrapped in 1956.

The next-to-last new cars came to the IT in the form of the Streamliners *in October, 1948. These were the first new cars since the 285 was delivered some 34 years previous. This "lead" car had four GE 1240A2 motors, was 66'10" long, but only weighed in at 9,000 pounds more than the 285. Probably the only comparable interurban cars in the same league were the CNS&M* Electroliners. *One thing is for sure. I never rode as fast in a Streamliner as I did on the Skokie Valley line in a "Liner."*

81

A sad photo taken through the fence, 300 rusts away in St. Louis in April, 1963. The cars never ran again after the IT abandoned passenger service on March 3, 1956. There were rumors (probably started by railfans) that the South Shore Line in Chicago was interested in buying two of the three-car Streamliner *trains, probably an advanced case of wishful thinking!* **(Earl Clark, Gordon Lloyd Collection)**

When I took this photo, parlor/diner 350 was "getting some sun" at the IT Springfield station in 1952. The reserved seat service had been dropped in September 1951 and the use of train names died at the same time. In addition to a number, this car had a name: "Louis Joliet" who was an early French explorer of the Illinois Valley and the Mississippi River.

The reserved seat coaches in service before the advent of the Streamliners were hard to find in the years following 1948. They had been bumped by the newer trains. Here we have located motorized trailer 510 at the Decatur Shop on June 24, 1950. She was built in 1911 by St. Louis Car and named MONTICELLO. Hyman-Michals, a scrap dealer in the area, cut her up five months after the photo was taken. Money from scrap helped offset the passenger losses on the ledgers, the traction world's method of "throwing the furniture on the fire!".

If my memory serves me correctly, I rode the cushions of IT 512, the CERRO GORDO, back in 1950, when it was a part of the BLUE TRAIN, filling in for an ailing Streamliner. At the time I could not afford the food service in the car, but I could handle the extra seat charge, which was 75 cents one way between the stations that I rode the car. It was a difficult choice to give up sitting on the right hand side with the motorman, in the baggage area (something included in the regular coach fare) or riding in luxury in the usually deserted parlor car, only having a side or rear facing view. St. Louis Car Company built this car also, in 1913. In 1952, the 512 was sold for scrap to Purdy and Company, another scrap dealer. Photo taken September 29, 1951.

Trailer car 532 was observed and photographed in the East Peoria yard on July 1, 1951. This splendid example of wood coach builders art was turned out by St. Louis Car Co. in 1911. It ran during WWII between Danville and Springfield. I recall seeing her in Champaign during the war when I was briefly stationed at Chanute Field with the Army Air Force.

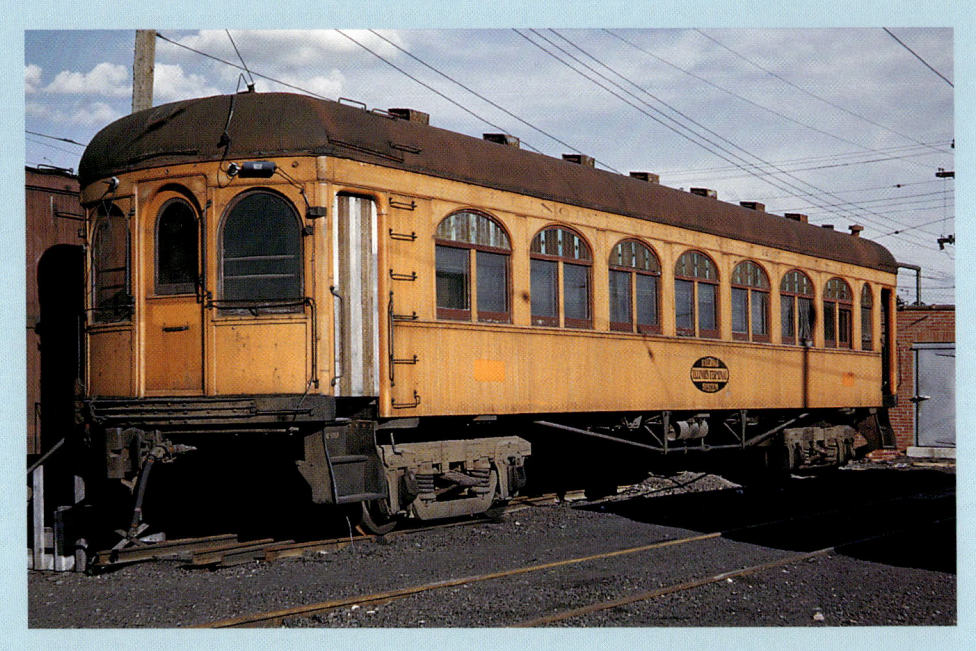

Trailer 528, minus trucks, is at Decatur. This car was a so-called "half-motor" as only one set of trucks was powered. The trucks have probably been dismantled for parts and the frames gone to scrap. In its prime, the car was air-conditioned, getting that treatment in 1937. A situation such as this scene might aptly be referred to as the "twilight zone!" **(Earl Clark, Gordon Lloyd Collection)**

IT 530, another half-motor was in service at Springfield when this view was taken on August 30, 1952. This car had received a new set of seats in the late '40s, and, surprisingly went through yet another interior-improvement rehab as late as 1953.

The Cincinnati Car Company constructed what became IT 601 in 1930 for the Cincinnati and Lake Erie Railroad. It was a freight motor when built, and as such it was the talk of the interurban community. C&LE interurban freight motors were usually recycled passenger cars. The company seldom ordered "new", but they took delivery of fifteen such units along with their infamous lightweight passenger cars the same year. Thus, this car was only nine years old when it was purchased by the IT. IT chose to de-motor the cars and make them express trailers. By September 29, 1951, she had received her coat of then standard blue and silver paint.

The orange version of a demotored C&LE freight motor posed at Springfield on June 8, 1952.

ELECTRIC LOCOMOTIVES

The roster of the IT, when it came to locomotives, covered the entire spectrum from steam to electric to diesel and even more exotic forms of power. One of the unique locomotives was 51, a hybrid electric-diesel-battery locomotive and originally a St. Louis Car Company demonstrator. The North Shore Line also operated this type of arrangement as did the Utah Copper Company. This locomotive was useful when operating in territory that was only partly under catenary. The battery portion of its power supply was removed in 1940. Normally seen in and about St. Louis, we found it this time at Springfield, on April 16, 1955, about six months before it was scrapped.

The pride and joy of the IT were the five Class "D" freight locomotives, 70-74. Built at the company shops in Decatur in 1940-42, they were streamlined in accordance with the 1940s state-of-the-art. In actuality, the streamlining merely disguised an ancient facade and covered up all of the ballast that made them heavier on the drivers. Originally painted traction orange, this loco was repainted in the green livery when seen at E. Peoria, on September 3, 1955.

Class "D"s looked better painted traction orange as this view of 73 at Springfield illustrates. The series 70-74 locomotives, all were rebuilt from Class "C" locos. This particular engine was once the 1584. In terms of locomotive weight, they tipped the scales at 97,000 lbs. heavier than a Class "C". To a locomotive, "weight" equals pulling power. To an electric passenger car, "weight" means slow acceleration, and high electric bills!

The work horse of IT electric freight power was the Class "B" loco. 1568, for example, was built in 1914 by the company shops in Decatur. Low light on September 29, 1951 at Springfield brings out the truck details nicely.

A green version of the Class "B" is seen at East Peoria on May 20, 1955. The green paint had been introduced by the PCC cars in 1949. In later years these locomotives were "bumped" from main line work and utilized as switchers in the IT classification yards.

87

In 1952, Class "C" 1587 was still painted in traction orange. She is "resting" at Champaign on this October day in 1953. About three years later she was sold for scrap to Compressed Steel Co.

Class "C" 1590 is at Decatur on September 3, 1955 wearing the original 1910 era olive green that is associated with this class of power. She had about one year of service left in here before going to the junk yard.

DIESEL LOCOMOTIVES

Alco S-2 700 waits a call to duty in East Alton on November 11, 1966. The unit was built in 1948 as replacement for steam power on non-electrified lines in the East St. Louis, ILL area and was renumbered 1001 in 1967 to correspond with its horsepower. It was traded in to EMD in 1970 on a new SW-1500.

A different look at an IT Alco S-2. 703 is on the turn-around tracks in the Midwest Terminal Building in St. Louis on July 1, 1951. This loco was traded to EMD in May, 1969 as credit for an SD-39. EMD may have reused the couplers, but little else.

In a paint style that would certainly show the dirt, 706 is at Madison on November 3, 1963. After being sold and resold several times, she wound up as an industrial unit at the Dominion Steel and Coal Co., a Canadian outfit.

706 had other "hues" in addition to the white with blue lettering shown previous. Here in the conventional color of the time, she waits at the Decatur Shop on an October day in 1953. IT stationed a diesel at Decatur long before the wires came down, because several industries there were not electrified. Repeated derailments on the Forsythe branch forced a return to electric freight motors.

Do you like RS-1s? Here is a beautiful example of what Alco could turn out back in 1950. It represented America's introduction to the road-switcher concept, years before EMD caught on and produced their GP-7. Seldom has 1,000 HP looked so good!

Then, on the other hand, an RS-1 could look a little "beat". 752 indeed does in this view at E. Alton on Armistice Day, November 11, 1966. By 1969, the RS-1s were being sold off to the GM&O.

GM&O 1052 makes no mystery of its previous owner in this April 1970 photo. After a stint on GM&O successor ICG, the boomer went east and became Green Mountain RR #400 in July 1976.

91

Three sevens would appear to be a lucky number, as this unit was sold to the N&W. She is shown at Springfield with IC 1075 in the background. This is about the same location where earlier in this volume, we saw IT electric cars and an IC 0-6-0 smoking away. The date, June 21, 1958, was one day prior to the very last IT passenger run, on the Granite City local.

Low western sun makes the running gear of the 778 clearly available for our inspection. The location is Madison, IL, in the greater St. Louis area, November 3, 1983. This SW-1200 packs 1,200 HP. It was sold to Archer Daniels Midland, at Peoria, in 1981.

My good friend Jim Buckley took this shot of IT 801, the road's only SW-8, at McKinley Junction, IL on September 20, 1969. Originally EMD demo 800, became IT #725 in 1951. The unit was renumbered 801 in 1967, and after acquisition by the N&W in 1981, it became their 2115. **(James Buckley, Gordon Lloyd Collection)**

1221 bearing the new style IT lettering is seen at Wood River, IL on November 29, 1980. These units had back-to-back MU capability.

Springfield is the location of 1506 with its train arriving from the north on April 5, 1981. Although the sun was fine at this particular time, subsequent photos taken on this date were taken with the sun playing "hide and seek."

A view of the IT Springfield diesel shop in twilight. GP-7 1506 (ex-1605) and a caboose grace the otherwise rundown facility o April 5, 1981. What was left of the IT was sold to the Norfolk and Western about a year later. By 1981, the IT was largely a trackage rights operation.

A resplendent 1502 shows off its brass bell at East Peoria on May 5, 1968. The fifteen year old was about as clean as they get. **(K.C. Henkels, Gordon Lloyd collection)**

Not so clean GP-7 1503 was "nailed" at Springfield in mid-Fall 1981. Her paint job a bit worse for the wear, she was a tireless work horse. After becoming N&W 3402, the unit was retired in 1984. **(Kevin Idarious, Gordon Lloyd collections)**

Looking down on a somewhat "rough" main line from the IT diesel shop in Springfield on April 5, 1981, we see GP-7 1506 and the nose of the 2002. GP-7 1605 is preserved at the Illinois Railway Museum.

95

Crossing the Sangamon River near Springfield on a less than ideal day, a five loco diesel "lashup" powers a freight. No sun, but I could just not let this string of diesels pass by without getting it on film.

GP-7s 1602 and 1604 are at the East Peoria shop building on a June day in 1959. One has to admit that this was a classic diesel paint scheme.

*"B" units on the IT? Yes it could and did happen. My friend Ray Bowlan shot this foursome near Decatur on May 20, 1968. One of the "B"s is still in its RF&P paint. This is indeed an unique photo. **(Ray Bowlan, Gordon Lloyd Collection)***

A short-lived company publication *Trains of Thought*, sought to build internal morale among IT employees. An example is this December 1977 issue. The wires were down for over 14 years, but there was still a railroad to run, and it required loyal workers. The company magazine sought to build the idea that the company was moving forward.

*SW-1500 #1513 at Granite City in January 1977 has had its lettering downgraded from the elaborate "Illinois Terminal to a simple "IT". **(Gordon Lloyd, Jr., Gordon Lloyd, Sr. Collection)***

97

The 2004 was an EMD GP38-2 photographed in January 1978 about 6 months after delivery. Soon, the "IT" was transformed into "NW" which to the railfan fraternity, stood for "Needs Washing!"

Jim Buckley drove hundreds of miles in Illinois as well as other states and countries, chasing railroads. We should all be grateful for his dedication. He has left us with many memorable photos like this "tank train" seen at Springfield on September 19, 1969. SD39's 2301-2303 ended up on the Boston & Maine after N&W purchased IT and found the unique SD's did not fit well in their "standardized" roster.
(James A. Buckley, Gordon Lloyd Collection)

ST. LOUIS AREA SUBURBAN CARS

IT 415 was one of a group of "nifty" suburban cars, built by St. Louis Car Company in 1924. There were 12 cars in the order. The initial owner was the IT subsidiary, the Chicago and Illinois Valley. After its sister cars went to scrap in 1956, the 415 was sent to the Illinois Railway Museum in Union. This shot was taken July 19, 1955 at Granite City.

There is a sales saying that you will get "two for the price of one". In this April 1, 1955 photo you get three for the price of one! The last three classes of suburban cars on IT are seen together at the Granite City barn. Do you have a favorite?

In regular service, on June 21, 1958, 473 crossed in front of PCC 454 at the apex of the figure 8 loop in downtown Granite City.

If only downtown Granite City looked this good today. In June, 1958, stores were still in operation, and business was flourishing, a natural dividend of cities served by trolley systems.

At Madison and 15th Streets in Granite City, the passage of PCC 451 was recorded on July 19, 1955. This car still operates at the Connecticut Electric Railway Museum and for a little over three years was on loan to the Shaker Heights Rapid Transit system in Cleveland.

Sad times. On June 21, 1958, two shop men posed for the photographer with a two-car PCC train heading for the St. Louis-Midwest Terminal building to be stored on basement tracks. Hopefully a buyer would appear. Alas, aside from the two PCCs sold to museums, the rest were scrapped.

Among the 1949 St. Louis Car Co. PCCs that went to the scrapper was 454. However, before that inglorious fate, this car was observed crossing GM&O trackage in Madison on June 21, 1958.

On the approach structure to the McKinley Bridge is 455 on a sunny day in Venice, IL, March 3, 1956. Venice is about 3 miles west of Granite City.

Coming off a viaduct over the TRRA in Venice is 454. Sharp eyes can locate TRRA 179, one of the last steamers on the TRRA in the left of the photo taken on April 16, 1955.

Running towards St. Louis, and powered by catenary strung from concrete poles, is car 473, which was destined to become the last "regular run" streetcar to operate in the state of Illinois. In fact, this is the last revenue day of the Granite City-St. Louis service, June 21, 1958. Streetcar service ended in Chicago about 18 hours earlier in the same service day giving the IT the championship.

Also operating in St. Louis on the last day was PCC 450. This car was later sold to the Ohio Railway Museum at Worthington, Ohio in 1964.

On the St. Louis elevated structure, 451 is about to cross over the Broadway car line of the St. Louis Public Service Co., on July 1, 1951.

Looking down on the turning track at Midwest Terminal as we did a few pages back on an IT interurban, we observe car 455 on July 1, 1951. It was resting in the general area that the PCCs were later stored for buyers who simply were not interested in the merchandise. The cars literally melted away there before they were finally cut up in 1964.

Thanks go to Earl Clark, for visiting St. Louis in early Spring, 1963 and turning his camera on this sad and dismal scene. The IT PCCs, once stored at Midwest Terminal, rest in a scrap yard in St. Louis prior to being cut up.
(Earl Clark, Gordon Lloyd Collection)

Your author rode the last IT trolley, 473, from St. Louis to the Granite City carbarn. The bad news, besides this being the last run, was that he did not have a tripod for his NIKON. This "fuzzball" shot was taken with the camera balanced on top of a fireplug making a time exposure at 1:00 AM, June 22, 1958.

WORK EQUIPMENT

The IT had a large variety of "work" and service equipment. We will not attempt in this volume to provide photographs of all of the many cars that IT used in support services. Many cars came and went before the advent of color film. Others were so elusive that luck was the only means by which they could be located and photographed. 09 as shown, was a wooden box car at one time. Now, with end doors cut in, and a stove inside, it is apparently a tool car at Decatur, June 22, 1958.

IT 020 is a bit easier to identify. It is obviously an ex-Class "B" locomotive made into a snow plow. It was number 1561 until December 9, 1955, when it assumed its new role. It was sold to the Chicago and Illinois Midland Railroad in 1959, then scrapped.

106

As 020 went, so did its mate, 021. It was the 1576 until transformed into a plow in December 1955. Rumor has it that several tons of cement were poured into the floor of this plow and 020 in order to give them greater stability in bucking snow drifts. Taken at Springfield on June 21, 1958.

Here we see the pair of snow plows, 020-021 at Springfield on February 16, 1956. **(Charles Able, Gordon Lloyd Collection)**

What's this? It would appear to be a portable fueling tank car for diesel locomotives. Numbered 023, it does not appear to be portable anymore. It is at Decatur on June 22, 1958.

At Springfield on August 20, 1959, 049 rests on a flawless summer day, in better times, it was sleeper 504, the PEORIA, built by ACF in 1914. Now she is designated as a "bunk car" for track crews during their off-duty hours away from home.

A publication frankly addressed to shippers was *Know Your Illinois*. It offered a map of the Illinois Terminal and history about the state. IT was ready to handle freight was the message.

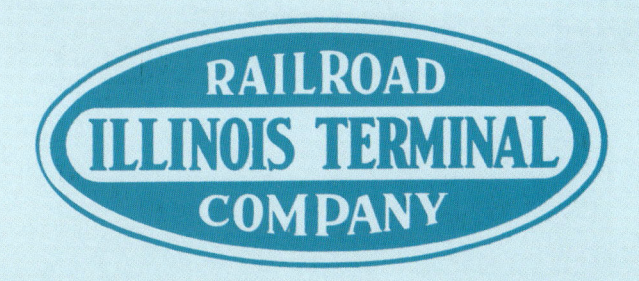

The sleeping car heritage can be noted in 050, seen at Wood River, on October 17, 1953. This car was formerly the interurban sleeper ST LOUIS. It was demoted to bunk service in December, 1939.

An outside braced box car, which in its declining days (June 14, 1959) was used in work service. Seen at Wood River.

058 is an example of the transformation of a proud C&LE freight motor moving down the pecking order to de-motored express trailer and finally to work status. Shown at Decatur, March 23, 1956.

Also at Decatur is another ex-C&LE freight motor, which seems to be even lower in status than 058. At least box car red paint gives the impression of lower lifestyle than the blue paint scheme.

081 was a combination car whose history is complex and practically untraceable. Obviously its final fate before scrapping was as a work car, shown here at Decatur on September 3, 1955.

111

At Wood River, on January 16, 1961, IT 049, formerly 504 PEORIA, a main line sleeping car is now a bunk car for maintenance of way workers. To say the least, she is in sad shape.

096 seems to have once been a coach, possibly a motor car. Those days were far behind as we viewed it at Lincoln.

No mistaking the fact that 097 was one of the thousands of "troop sleepers" built during World War II by Pullman. Troops called them "side door Pullmans." The war has been over for 13 years as we observe it in service. Aside from the side door being welded shut, and the boxcar red paint job, it looks like it did when it was in its intended service. Wood River, June 22, 1958.

Appearing in better condition than other service cars is 0100, an Instruction Car at Wood River, September 19, 1954. This car was formerly 518 when in passenger service and was demoted on December 31, 1952. It was built by St. Louis Car in 1911.

1700 was built at Decatur Shop in 1907 and like most IT Line Cars, spent a lot of time standing still awaiting calls to repair the overhead wire. She is painted in the color of the "old order" at Danville on April 20, 1952.

We view 1702 in a different perspective than 1700. Time is now June, 1955, and IT line cars tend to be boxcar red. Scene is at Granite City on June 21, 1958. The 1702 was sold to the Illinois Railway Museum in October, 1958.

FREIGHT CARS AND CABOOSES

INSULATED BOX CARS

The IT was an active freight carrier, interchanging freight cars with other railroads in the US. As late as 1980, it had 2,713 cars in flat, covered hopper and box configurations which carried IT markings. One of these was RBL insulated car series 900-912. She is in a Conrail train passing Leetsdale, PA on October 21, 1978.

FLAT CARS

IT flat car 1312 coupled to NS 30894 at Tolono, IL on the old WABASH trackage on January 11, 1984. (Kevin Idarious, Gordon Lloyd Collection)

COVERED HOPPERS

Covered hoppers were important to the IT, more than other carriers its size, as IT probably had more grain elevators along its tracks than similar sized railroads. 1927 was shot at Decatur on July 18, 1974.

This LO style covered hopper, one of 977 cars in the group, was noted and photographed at Harrisonburg, VA on the Chesapeake Western Railway in early 1982.

BOX CARS

Illinois Terminal Railroad Company

IT 8151 is in the Conway yard of Conrail (former PRR) on August 20, 1987. This XM style box car has a cushioned underframe.
(Gordon Lloyd, Jr., Gordon Lloyd, Sr. Collection)

Of another age is IT 8167, a 40' outside braced wooden box car. At one time there were thousands of these cars in service on US railroads. As you can see, this car was restricted to "on line" service between Federal, IL., Springfield, and Decatur as of July 16, 1961.

An IT box car of XM classification was 8415, one of a group of 54. This view is at Decatur on July 18, 1974.

A brochure prepared for major shippers was the spiral bound Progress Report. It was given to those invited to a dinner hosted by the President of the IT. I received this copy when I was Western Area Traffic Manager for United States Steel Corp. The IT put on its best face at such occasions. Shippers were given a view of IT capabilities in handling freight. In 1970, the IT was raring to go as an independent carrier.

Progress Report

116

1970

CABOOSES

The IT possessed many types of caboose. One of the short kind was 061, which saw service in the Wood River area on June 22, 1958.

A switching "hack", was the 805 seen at East Peoria on August 22, 1959. Nice red paint, although the car was still fairly new, having been built in 1945.

An "assigned" caboose with a bay window 971 was only used in Decatur at the time this photo was made, February 14, 1981. (Gary Powell, Gordon Lloyd Collection)

Very "main line" in appearance, is caboose 981, at Springfield on June 16, 1961.

Cabooses should be red, and this one, 982, indeed is. It was built by St. Louis Car Company in 1953. We see it at McKinley Junction, IL on January 6, 1954. Little did we realize that some day cabooses would also become an endangered species like the interurban!

A refugee is this unnumbered IT caboose displayed at Girard on August 31, 1993. A memorial of sorts, to a line that did so much for the town where it now rests.

POTPOURRI

Potpourri, has been defined by Webster to mean "miscellaneous collection". The slides that follow do meet that criteria. The IT was vastly more complex than other Illinois traction properties. Considering its close community of interest with the Illinois Power Company, it was not unusual that IT locomotive were sold to Illinois Power for use in moving coal to power generating facilities. In this view, a former IT Class "A" locomotive is seen at the power house in Bloomington on June 22, 1958. The tracks have been covered over with earth indicating that trucks are currently bringing the coal into this facility.

The oldest ITC time table in my collection is an interesting issue dated March 7, 1926. Among its unique features is a system map showing the Staunton-Hillsboro Branch, the Danville-Ridge Farm line and the complete Illinois Valley Div. Comprehensive time schedules inside show a busy Peoria to St. Louis main line with 12 passenger runs each way, plus four Springfield Round trips. Interest was generated in illustrations of the comforts of Parlor Car and Sleeping Car travel on ITC. When issued, this timetable was in the pocket of most businessmen and many "just folks" as the interurban was the way to travel in Illinois.

Illinois Traction System

Fast~Frequent Passenger Trains

BETWEEN

St. Louis	Peoria
Edwardsville	Decatur
Staunton	Champaign
Litchfield	Urbana
Hillsboro	Danville
Carlinville	Lincoln
Springfield	Bloomington

AND INTERMEDIATE POINTS

BOOK of TRAINS

EFFECTIVE MARCH 7, 1926

MAIN DIVISION

A four-car IT train is being "hauled" over trackage without wire in this view at Edwardsville on September 19, 1954. The abandonment of IT passenger service, although rumored at the time, was still considered by many to be unthinkable!

On the same day as the preceding photo, we find the same special train at Alton on the freight line. The fans are everywhere!

A postcard shot, showing a Class "B" motor with a flock of IT boxcars trailing it. Good copy but one would seldom see such a scene in regular day-to-day service.

No, this is not a photograph. Rather, it is a water color painting made from one of my slides. The noted artist, Mr. Stanley Cook, of Westwood, MA has interpreted my work into a "softer" and perhaps more appealing view of an IT train at Ogden.

It was mentioned earlier in this volume that IT sold one of its PCCs to the Ohio Railway Museum, near Columbus. We see 450 at Worthington, Ohio on May 9, 1975. This car too saw service between 1976 and 1979 on the Shaker Heights line in Cleveland while new cars were on order there.

The only view of the Chicago, Ottawa and Peoria in this volume is this view of the CO&P station in Morris, IL taken by Don Idarious on July 13, 1990. Besides being a substation in the IT tradition the station was also used by the Fox and Illinois Union, an interurban line that struggled on until 1938 or so, between Aurora and Morris, IL. That operation used a former electric freight motor that had been converted to a gas-electric. **(Donald Idarious, Gordon Lloyd Collection)**

123

On a visit to Champaign from my hometown, Chicago, I heard a lot of noise coming from the nearby Illinois Power Company generating station. Walking over to the facility, I found that the motorman of IPC 1 (a former IT Class "A" loco) was inside the hopper car beating on it with a sledge hammer. I doubt if the B&O would have appreciated the damage he was doing to the car while trying to dislodge the coal on October 17, 1953.

About 2 1/2 years later, a Class "B" locomotive purchased from the IT was at the Champaign power house. It was numbered 90535, numbered in the series of the motor trucks and other IPC service equipment on March 23, 1956.

If something seems wrong with this view it is that the two IT cars seen near the former IT station in Champaign, IL, 233 and 234, are static exhibits. Both cars are now at the Illinois Railway Museum at Union, IL. Photo was taken on August 31, 1957.

126

At Barrett, MO on May 15, 1989, an IT Class "C" is seen in approximation of its former glory. In its operating days, this baby moved a lot of freight for its owner.

April 26, 1953, the IT timetable still has a *Streamliner* on its cover, however all "name" passenger runs and reserved seat coaches have been discontinued. Three trains a day run on the abbreviated "Danville" line. The original "main line, via Bloomington has been abandoned.

127

The IT Champaign-Springfield line swings lazily across Illinois State Route 10, just west of Champaign. It is a dismal day. Such days never bothered the "hot" schedules of the IT. Rain or shine, IT trains generally kept to their schedules.

illinois terminal

Writing this volume on the Illinois Terminal has brought back many memories of the railroad. Riding up front in the conventional cars, sitting there to the right of the motorman, and watching the trolley wire support poles whiz by like pickets in a wood fence. On other trips, luxuriating in the reserved seat coach, sipping a beverage and being catered to by a courteous attendant, even such mundane sights as watching how efficiently baggage and express was handled. All were marks of a dedicated team, one of the reasons that the Traction was long-lived. However, this will be merely one volume of a projected two-volume study of the Traction. My good friend Eugene Van Dusen will offer his work in Volume II on the line. Readers who obtain both volumes will be able to see the property from two different perspectives. This work covers the ITC from 1950 until the Norfolk and Western took control of the line on May 8, 1982. Van's coverage will be 100% electric and will intensively cover the Traction in the 1950s. An electric railroad of the character of the ITC deserves two different appraisals. We hope you have enjoyed Volume I of the *Illinois Terminal in Color*, and urge you to also purchase Volume II.